SECOND EDITION

Java 7 Pocket Guide

Robert Liguori and Patricia Liguori

O'REILLY®

Beijing · Cambridge · Farnham · Köln · Sebastopol · Tokyo

Java 7 Pocket Guide, Second Edition

by Robert Liguori and Patricia Liguori

Copyright © 2013 Gliesian, LLC. All rights reserved.

Printed in the United States of America.

Published by O'Reilly Media, Inc., 1005 Gravenstein Highway North, Sebastopol, CA 95472.

O'Reilly books may be purchased for educational, business, or sales promotional use. Online editions are also available for most titles (*http://my.safaribooksonline.com*). For more information, contact our corporate/institutional sales department: 800-998-9938 or *corporate@oreilly.com*.

Editors: Mike Loukides and Meghan Blanchette
Production Editor: Rachel Steely
Copyeditor: Jasmine Kwityn
Proofreader: Charles Roumeliotis
Indexer: Ellen Troutman
Cover Designer: Randy Comer
Interior Designer: David Futato
Illustrator: Rebecca Demarest

July 2013:   Second Edition

Revision History for the Second Edition:

    2013-07-03:   First release
    2013-08-02:   Second release
    2013-10-25:   Third release

See *http://oreilly.com/catalog/errata.csp?isbn=9781449343569* for release details.

ISBN: 978-1-449-34356-9

[LSI]

This book is dedicated to our beautiful, awesome-tastic daughter, Ashleigh.

Table of Contents

Preface   xi

Part I.   Language

Chapter 1: Naming Conventions   3
    Class Names   3
    Interface Names   3
    Method Names   4
    Instance and Static Variable Names   4
    Parameter and Local Variable Names   4
    Generic Type Parameter Names   4
    Constant Names   5
    Enumeration Names   5
    Package Names   5
    Acronyms   6

Chapter 2: Lexical Elements   7
    Unicode and ASCII   7
    Comments   9
    Keywords   10

Identifiers   11
Separators   12
Operators   12
Literals   13
Escape Sequences   16
Unicode Currency Symbols   17

Chapter 3: Fundamental Types   **19**
Primitive Types   19
Literals for Primitive Types   20
Floating-Point Entities   21
Numeric Promotion of Primitive Types   24
Wrapper Classes   25
Autoboxing and Unboxing   26

Chapter 4: Reference Types   **29**
Comparing Reference Types to Primitive Types   30
Default Values   30
Conversion of Reference Types   32
Converting Between Primitives and Reference Types   33
Passing Reference Types into Methods   33
Comparing Reference Types   35
Copying Reference Types   38
Memory Allocation and Garbage Collection of
        Reference Types   39

Chapter 5: Object-Oriented Programming   **41**
Classes and Objects   41
Variable-Length Argument Lists   47
Abstract Classes and Abstract Methods   49
Static Data Members, Static Methods, Static Constants, and
        Static Initializers   50

Interfaces   51
Enumerations   52
Annotation Types   53

Chapter 6: Statements and Blocks   **55**
Expression Statements   55
Empty Statement   56
Blocks   56
Conditional Statements   56
Iteration Statements   58
Transfer of Control   60
Synchronized Statement   62
Assert Statement   62
Exception Handling Statements   63

Chapter 7: Exception Handling   **65**
The Exception Hierarchy   65
Checked/Unchecked Exceptions and Errors   66
Common Checked/Unchecked Exceptions and Errors   67
Exception Handling Keywords   69
The Exception Handling Process   74
Defining Your Own Exception Class   75
Printing Information About Exceptions   75

Chapter 8: Java Modifiers   **79**
Access Modifiers   80
Other (Nonaccess) Modifiers   81

Part II.   Platform

Chapter 9: Java Platform, SE   **85**

Common Java SE API Libraries   86

Chapter 10: Development Basics   **99**
    Java Runtime Environment   99
    Java Development Kit   99
    Java Program Structure   100
    Command-Line Tools   102
    Classpath   109

Chapter 11: Memory Management   **111**
    Garbage Collectors   111
    Memory Management Tools   113
    Command-Line Options   114
    Resizing the JVM Heap   117
    Interfacing with the GC   117

Chapter 12: Basic Input and Output   **119**
    Standard Streams in, out, and err   119
    Class Hierarchy for Basic Input and Output   120
    File Reading and Writing   121
    Socket Reading and Writing   123
    Serialization   124
    Zipping and Unzipping Files   126
    File and Directory Handling   127

Chapter 13: NIO 2.0 Quicklook   **129**
    The Path Interface   129
    The Files Class   130
    Additional Features   131

Chapter 14: Concurrency   **133**
    Creating Threads   133

Thread States	134
Thread Priorities	135
Common Methods	135
Synchronization	136
Concurrent Utilities	138

Chapter 15: Java Collections Framework   **143**

The Collection Interface	143
Implementations	144
Collection Framework Methods	144
Collections Class Algorithms	145
Algorithm Efficiencies	146
Comparator Interface	147

Chapter 16: Generics Framework   **149**

Generic Classes and Interfaces	149
Constructors with Generics	150
Substitution Principle	151
Type Parameters, Wildcards, and Bounds	152
The Get and Put Principle	152
Generic Specialization	154
Generic Methods in Raw Types	154

Chapter 17: The Java Scripting API   **157**

Scripting Languages	157
Script Engine Implementations	157
Setting Up Scripting Languages and Engines	160

Part III. Appendixes

A. Third-Party Tools   **165**

B. UML Basics   175

Index   185

Preface

Designed to be your companion in the office, in the lab, or even on the road, this *Pocket Guide* provides a quick reference to the standard features of the Java programming language and its platform.

This *Pocket Guide* provides you with the information you will need while developing or debugging your Java programs, including helpful programming examples, tables, figures, and lists.

It also contains supplemental information about things such as the Java Scripting API, third-party tools, and the basics of the Unified Modeling Language (UML).

Java coverage in this book has been updated for new features through Java SE 7, including basic information on NIO 2.0, the G1 Garbage Collector, and JSR 334: Small Language Enhancements (Project Coin). Project Coin enhancements include improved literals (e.g., use of the underscore character), the new (generics-related) diamond operator, and exception handling extensions (e.g., the new multi-catch and try-with-resources statements).

The material in this book also provides support in preparing for the Oracle Certified Associate Java SE 7 Programmer I Exam. If you are considering pursuing this Java certification, you may also wish to consider acquiring *OCA Java SE 7 Programmer I Study Guide (Exam 1Z0-803)* by Edward Finegan and Robert Liguori (McGraw-Hill Osborne Media, 2012).

Book Structure

This book is broken into three parts: Language, Platform, and Appendixes. Chapters 1 through 8 detail the Java programming language as derived from the Java Language Specification (JLS). Chapters 9 through 17 detail Java platform components and related topics. The appendixes cover third-party tools and the Unified Modeling Language.

Conventions Used in This Book

The following typographical conventions are used in this book:

Italic
>   Indicates new terms, URLs, email addresses, filenames, and file extensions.

`Constant width`
>   Used for program listings, as well as within paragraphs to refer to program elements such as variable or function names, databases, data types, environment variables, statements, and keywords.

`Constant width italic`
>   Shows text that should be replaced with user-supplied values or by values determined by context.

Authors

Robert Liguori is a senior software engineer for Solentus (*http://www.solentus.com*). He is an Oracle Certified Expert, supporting several Java-based air traffic management applications. Patricia

Liguori is a multi-disciplinary information systems engineer for The MITRE Corporation (*http://www.mitre.org/*). She has been developing real-time air traffic management systems and aviation related information systems since 1994.

Safari® Books Online

NOTE

Safari Books Online (*www.safaribooksonline.com*) is an on-demand digital library that delivers expert content in both book and video form from the world's leading authors in technology and business.

Technology professionals, software developers, web designers, and business and creative professionals use Safari Books Online as their primary resource for research, problem solving, learning, and certification training.

Safari Books Online offers a range of product mixes and pricing programs for organizations, government agencies, and individuals. Subscribers have access to thousands of books, training videos, and prepublication manuscripts in one fully searchable database from publishers like O'Reilly Media, Prentice Hall Professional, Addison-Wesley Professional, Microsoft Press, Sams, Que, Peachpit Press, Focal Press, Cisco Press, John Wiley & Sons, Syngress, Morgan Kaufmann, IBM Redbooks, Packt, Adobe Press, FT Press, Apress, Manning, New Riders, McGraw-Hill, Jones & Bartlett, Course Technology, and dozens more. For more information about Safari Books Online, please visit us online.

How to Contact Us

Please address comments and questions concerning this book to the publisher:

O'Reilly Media, Inc.
1005 Gravenstein Highway North
Sebastopol, CA 95472
800-998-9938 (in the United States or Canada)
707-829-0515 (international or local)
707-829-0104 (fax)

We have a web page for this book, where we list errata, examples, and any additional information. You can access this page at *http://oreil.ly/Java7_Pkt*.

To comment or ask technical questions about this book, send email to *bookquestions@oreilly.com*.

For more information about our books, courses, conferences, and news, see our website at *http://www.oreilly.com*.

Find us on Facebook: *http://facebook.com/oreilly*

Follow us on Twitter: *http://twitter.com/oreillymedia*

Watch us on YouTube: *http://www.youtube.com/oreillymedia*

Second Edition Acknowledgments

We extend a special thank you to our editor, Meghan Blanchette. Her oversight and collaboration has been invaluable in the endeavor. In this regard, we are very happy with the various improvements, errata updates, and Java SE 7 coverage that we have been able to include in this update.

Further appreciation goes out to our technical reviewers, Ryan Cuprak and Jonathan S. Weissman, as well as the various members of the O'Reilly team, our family, and our friends.

We would also like to thank again all of those who participated with the 1st Edition of the book.

PART I

Language

CHAPTER 2

Lexical Elements

Java source code consists of words or symbols called lexical elements or tokens. Java lexical elements include line terminators, whitespace, comments, keywords, identifiers, separators, operators, and literals. The words or symbols in the Java programming language are comprised of the Unicode character set.

Unicode and ASCII

Maintained by the Unicode Consortium standards organization, Unicode is the universal character set with the first 128 characters being the same as those in the American Standard Code for Information Interchange (ASCII) character set. Unicode provides a unique number for every character, usable across all platforms, programs, and languages. Java SE 7 uses Unicode 6.0.0 and you can find more about it in the online manual (*http://bit.ly/16mhEDL*). Java SE 6 and J2SE 5.0 use Unicode 4.0.

TIP

Java comments, identifiers, and string literals are not limited to ASCII characters. All other Java input elements are formed from ASCII characters.

The Unicode set version used by a specified version of the Java platform is documented in the Character class of the Java API. The Unicode Character Code Chart for scripts, symbols, and punctuation can be accessed at *http://unicode.org/charts/*.

Printable ASCII Characters

ASCII reserves code 32 (spaces) and codes 33 to 126 (letters, digits, punctuation marks, and a few others) for printable characters. Table 2-1 contains the decimal values followed by the corresponding ASCII characters for these codes.

Table 2-1. Printable ASCII characters

32 SP	48 0	64 @	80 P	96 '	112 p
33 !	49 1	65 A	81 Q	97 a	113 q
34 "	50 2	66 B	82 R	98 b	114 r
35 #	51 3	67 C	83 S	99 c	115 s
36 $	52 4	68 D	84 T	100 d	116 t
37 %	53 5	69 E	85 U	101 e	117 u
38 &	54 6	70 F	86 V	102 f	118 v
39 '	55 7	71 G	87 W	103 g	119 w
40 (	56 8	72 H	88 X	104 h	120 x
41)	57 9	73 I	89 Y	105 i	121 y
42 *	58 :	74 J	90 Z	106 j	122 z
43 +	59 ;	75 K	91 [	107 k	123 {
44 ,	60 <	76 L	92 \	108 l	124	
45 -	61 =	77 M	93]	109 m	125 }
46 .	62 >	78 N	94 ^	110 n	126 ~
47 /	63 ?	79 O	95 _	111 o	

Nonprintable ASCII Characters

ASCII reserves decimal numbers 0–31 and 127 for *control characters*. Table 2-2 contains the decimal values followed by the corresponding ASCII characters for these codes.

Table 2-2. Nonprintable ASCII characters

00 NUL	07 BEL	14 SO	21 NAK	28 FS
01 SOH	08 BS	15 SI	22 SYN	29 GS
02 STX	09 HT	16 DLE	23 ETB	30 RS
03 ETX	10 NL	17 DC1	24 CAN	31 US
04 EOT	11 VT	18 DC2	25 EM	127 DEL
05 ENQ	12 NP	19 DC3	26 SUB	
06 ACK	13 CR	20 DC4	27 ESC	

TIP

ASCII 10 is a newline or linefeed. ASCII 13 is a carriage return.

Comments

A single-line comment begins with two forward slashes and ends immediately before the line terminator character:

```
// A comment on a single line
```

A multiline comment begins with a forward slash, immediately followed by an asterisk, and ends with an asterisk immediately followed by a forward slash. The single asterisks in between provide a nice formatting convention; they are typically used, but are not required:

```
/*
 * A comment that can span multiple lines
 * just like this
 */
```

A Javadoc comment is processed by the Javadoc tool to generate API documentation in HTML format. A Javadoc comment must begin with a forward slash, immediately followed by two asterisks, and end with an asterisk immediately followed by a forward slash (Oracle's documentation page (*http://bit.ly/16mhGeT*) provides more information on the Javadoc tool):

```
/** This is my Javadoc comment */
```

In Java, comments cannot be nested:

```
/* This is /* not permissible */ in Java */
```

Keywords

Table 2-3 contains the Java keywords. Two of these, the const and goto keywords, are reserved but are not used by the Java language. Java 5.0 introduced the enum keyword.

TIP

Java keywords cannot be used as identifiers in a Java program.

Table 2-3. Java keywords

abstract	double	int	super
assert	else	interface	switch
boolean	enum	long	synchronized
break	extends	native	this
byte	final	new	throw
case	finally	package	throws
catch	float	private	transient
char	for	protected	try
class	if	public	void

const	goto	return	volatile
continue	implements	short	while
default	import	static	
do	instanceof	strictfp	

TIP

Sometimes `true`, `false`, and `null` literals are mistaken for keywords. They are not keywords; they are reserved literals.

Identifiers

A Java identifier is the name that a programmer gives to a class, method, variable, and so on.

Identifiers cannot have the same Unicode character sequence as any keyword, `boolean`, or null literal.

Java identifiers are made up of Java letters. A Java letter is a character for which `Character.isJavaIdentifierStart(int)` returns `true`. Java letters from the ASCII character set are limited to the dollar sign ($), the underscore symbol (_), and upper- and lowercase letters.

Digits are also allowed in identifiers, but *after* the first character:

```
// Valid identifier examples
class TestDriver {...}
String testVariable;
int _testVariable;
Long $testVariable;
startTest(testVariable1);
```

See Chapter 1 for naming guidelines.

Separators

Twelve ASCII characters delimit program parts and are used as separators. (), { }, and [ ] are used in pairs:

```
( ) { } [ ] < > : ; , .
```

Operators

Operators perform operations on one, two, or three operands and return a result. Operator types in Java include assignment, arithmetic, comparison, bitwise, increment/decrement, and class/object. Table 2-4 contains the Java operators listed in precedence order (those with the highest precedence at the top of the table), along with a brief description of the operators and their associativity (left to right or right to left).

Table 2-4. Java operators

Precedence	Operator	Description	Association
1	++,--	Postincrement, postdecrement	R → L
2	++,--	Preincrement, predecrement	R → L
	+,-	Unary plus, unary minus	R → L
	~	Bitwise complement	R → L
	!	Boolean NOT	R → L
3	new	Create object	R → L
	(type)	Type cast	R → L
4	*,/,%	Multiplication, division, remainder	L → R
5	+,-	Addition, subtraction	L → R
	+	String concatenation	L → R
6	<<, >>, >>>	Left shift, right shift, unsigned right shift	L → R
7	<, <=, >, >=	Less than, less than or equal to, greater than, greater than or equal to	L → R

Precedence	Operator	Description	Association
	instanceof	Type comparison	L → R
8	==, !=	Value equality and inequality	L → R
	==, !=	Reference equality and inequality	L → R
9	&	Boolean AND	L → R
	&	Bitwise AND	L → R
10	^	Boolean exclusive OR (XOR)	L → R
	^	Bitwise exclusive OR (XOR)	L → R
11	|	Boolean inclusive OR	L → R
	|	Bitwise inclusive OR	L → R
12	&&	Logical AND (a.k.a. conditional AND)	L → R
13	||	Logical OR (a.k.a. conditional OR)	L → R
14	?:	Conditional ternary operator	L → R
15	=, +=, -=, *=, /=, %=, &=, ^=, |=, <<=, >> =, >>>=	Assignment operators	R → L

Literals

Literals are source code representation of values. As of Java SE 7, underscores are allowed in numeric literals to enhance readability of the code. The underscores may only be placed between individual numbers, and are ignored at runtime.

For more information on primitive type literals, see "Literals for Primitive Types" on page 20 in Chapter 3.

Boolean Literals

Boolean literals are expressed as either true or false:

```
boolean isReady = true;
boolean isSet = new Boolean(false); // unboxed
boolean isGoing = false;
```

Character Literals

A character literal is either a single character or an escape sequence contained within single quotes. Line terminators are not allowed:

```
char charValue1 = 'a';
// An apostrophe
Character charValue2 = new Character ('\'');
```

Integer Literals

Integer types (byte, short, int, and long) can be expressed in decimal, hexadecimal, octal, and binary. By default, integer literals are of type int:

```
int intValue1 = 34567, intValue2 = 1_000_000;
```

Decimal integers contain any number of ASCII digits zero through nine and represent positive numbers:

```
Integer integerValue1 = new Integer(100);
```

Prefixing the decimal with the unary negation operator can form a negative decimal:

```
publis static final int INT_VALUE = -200;
```

Hexadecimal literals begin with 0x or 0X, followed by the ASCII digits zero through nine and the letters a through f (or A through F). Java is *not* case-sensitive when it comes to hexadecimal literals.

Hex numbers can represent positive and negative integers and zero:

```
int intValue3 = 0X64; // 100 decimal from hex
```

Octal literals begin with a zero followed by one or more ASCII digits zero through seven:

```
int intValue4 = 0144; // 100 decimal from octal
```

Binary literals are expressed using the prefix 0b or 0B followed by zeros and ones:

```
char msgValue1 = 0b01001111; // O
char msgValue2 = 0B01001011; // K
char msgValue3 = 0B0010_0001; // !
```

To define an integer as type long, suffix it with an ASCII letter L (preferred and more readable) or l:

```
long longValue = 100L;
```

Floating-Point Literals

A valid floating-point literal requires a whole number and/or a fractional part, decimal point, and type suffix. An exponent prefaced by an e or E is optional. Fractional parts and decimals are not required when exponents or type suffixes are applied.

A floating-point literal (double) is a double-precision floating point of eight bytes. A float is four bytes. Type suffixes for doubles are d or D; suffixes for floats are f or F:

```
[whole-number].[fractional_part][e|E exp][f|F|d|D]

float floatValue1 = 9.15f, floatValue2 = 1_168f;
Float floatValue3 = new Float(20F);
double doubleValue1 = 3.12;
Double doubleValue2 = new Double(1e058);
float expValue1 = 10.0e2f, expValue2=10.0E3f;
```

String Literals

String literals contain zero or more characters, including escape sequences enclosed in a set of double quotes. String literals cannot contain Unicode \u000a and \u000d for line terminators; use \r and \n instead. Strings are immutable:

```
String stringValue1 = new String("Valid literal.");
String stringValue2 = "Valid.\nOn new line.";
String stringValue3 = "Joins str" + "ings";
String stringValue4 = "\"Escape Sequences\"\r";
```

There is a pool of strings associated with class String. Initially, the pool is empty. Literal strings and string-valued constant expressions are interned in the pool and added to the pool only once.

The following example shows how literals are added to and used in the pool:

```
// Adds String "thisString" to the pool
String stringValue5 = "thisString";
// Uses String "thisString" from the pool
String stringValue6 = "thisString";
```

A string can be added to the pool (if it does not already exist in the pool) by calling the intern() method on the string. The intern() method returns a string, which is either a reference to the new string that was added to the pool or a reference to the already existing string:

```
String stringValue7 = new String("thatString");
String stringValue8 = stringValue7.intern();
```

Null Literals

The null literal is of type null and can be applied to reference types. It does not apply to primitive types:

```
String n = null;
```

Escape Sequences

Table 2-5 provides the set of escape sequences in Java.

Table 2-5. Character and string literal escape sequences

Name	Sequence	Decimal	Unicode
Backspace	\b	8	\u0008
Horizontal tab	\t	9	\u0009
Line feed	\n	10	\u000A
Form feed	\f	12	\u000C
Carriage return	\r	13	\u000D

Name	Sequence	Decimal	Unicode
Double quote	\"	34	\u0022
Single quote	\'	39	\u0027
Backslash	\\	92	\u005C

Different line terminators are used for different platforms to achieve a newline; see Table 2-6. The println() method, which includes a line break, is a better solution than hardcoding \n and \r, when used appropriately.

Table 2-6. Newline variations

Operating system	Newline
POSIX-compliant operating systems (e.g., Solaris, Linux) and Mac OS X	LF (\n)
Mac OS up to version 9	CR (\r)
Microsoft Windows	CR+LF (\r\n)

Unicode Currency Symbols

Unicode currency symbols are present in the range of \u20A0–\u20CF (8352–8399). See Table 2-7 for examples.

Table 2-7. Currency symbols within range

Name	Symbol	Decimal	Unicode
Franc sign	₣	8355	\u20A3
Lira sign	₤	8356	\u20A4
Mill sign	₥	8357	\u20A5
Rupee sign	₨	8360	\u20A8
Dong sign	₫	8363	\u20AB
Euro sign	€	8364	\u20AC
Drachma sign	₯	8367	\u20AF
German penny sign	₰	8368	\u20B0

A number of currency symbols exist outside of the designated currency range. See Table 2-8 for examples.

Table 2-8. Currency symbols outside of range

Name	Symbol	Decimal	Unicode
Dollar sign	$	36	\u0024
Cent sign	¢	162	\u00A2
Pound sign	£	163	\u00A3
Currency sign	¤	164	\u00A4
Yen sign	¥	165	\u00A5
Yen/Yuan variant	圓	22278	\u5706

CHAPTER 3

Fundamental Types

Fundamental types include the Java primitive types and their corresponding wrapper classes/reference types. Java 5.0 and beyond provide for automatic conversion between these primitive and reference types through autoboxing and unboxing. Numeric promotion is applied to primitive types where appropriate.

Primitive Types

There are eight primitive types in Java; each is a reserved keyword. They describe variables that contain single values of the appropriate format and size; see Table 3-1. Primitive types are always the specified precision, regardless of the underlying hardware precisions (e.g., 32- or 64-bit).

Table 3-1. Primitive types

Type	Detail	Storage	Range
boolean	true or false	1 bit	Not applicable
char	Unicode character	2 bytes	\u0000 to \uFFFF
byte	Integer	1 byte	−128 to 127
short	Integer	2 bytes	−32768 to 32767
int	Integer	4 bytes	−2147483648 to 2147483647
long	Integer	8 bytes	-2^{63} to $2^{63} -1$

Type	Detail	Storage	Range
float	Floating point	4 bytes	$1.4e^{-45}$ to $3.4e^{+38}$
double	Floating point	8 bytes	$5e^{-324}$ to $1.8e^{+308}$

TIP

Primitive types byte, short, int, long, float, and double are all signed. Type char is unsigned.

Literals for Primitive Types

All primitive types, except boolean, can accept character, decimal, hexadecimal, octal, and Unicode literal formats, as well as character escape sequences. Where appropriate, the literal value is automatically cast or converted. Remember that bits are lost during truncation. The following is a list of primitive assignment examples:

```
boolean isTitleFight = true;
```
> The boolean primitive's only valid literal values are true and false.

```
char[] cArray = {'\u004B', 'O', '\'', 0x0064, 041,(char)
131105, 0b00100001}; // KO'd!!!
```
> The char primitive represents a single Unicode character. Literal values of the char primitive that are greater than two bytes need to be explicitly cast.

```
byte rounds = 12, fighters = (byte) 2;
```
> The byte primitive has a four-byte signed integer as its valid literal. If an explicit cast is not performed, the integer is implicitly cast to one byte.

```
short seatingCapacity = 17157, vipSeats = (short) 500;
```
> The short primitive has a four-byte signed integer as its valid literal. If an explicit cast is not performed, the integer is implicitly cast to two bytes.

```
int ppvRecord = 19800000, vs = vipSeats, venues = (int)
20000.50D;
```
The int primitive has a four-byte signed integer as its valid literal. When char, byte, and short primitives are used as literals, they are automatically cast to four-byte integers, as in the case of the short value within vipSeats. Floating-point and long literals must be explicitly cast.

```
long wins = 38L, losses = 4l, draws = 0, knockouts =
(long) 30;
```
The long primitive uses an eight-byte signed integer as its valid literal. It is designated by an L or l postfix. The value is cast from four bytes to eight bytes when no postfix or cast is applied.

```
float payPerView = 54.95F, balcony = 200.00f, ringside =
(float) 2000, cheapSeats = 50;
```
The float primitive has a four-byte signed floating point as its valid literal. An F or f postfix or an explicit cast designates it. No explicit cast is necessary for an int literal because an int fits in a float.

```
double champsPay = 20000000.00D, challengersPay =
12000000.00d, chlTrainerPay = (double) 1300000, referee
sPay = 3000, soda = 4.50;
```
The double primitive uses an eight-byte signed floating-point value as its valid literal. The literal can have a D, d, or explicit cast with no postfix. If the literal is an integer, it is implicitly cast.

See Chapter 2 for more details on literals.

Floating-Point Entities

Positive and negative floating-point infinities, negative zero, and Not-a-Number (NaN) are special entities defined to meet the IEEE 754-1985 standard; see Table 3-2.

The Infinity, -Infinity, and -0.0 entities are returned when an operation creates a floating-point value that is too large to be traditionally represented.

Table 3-2. Floating-point entities

Entity	Description	Examples
Infinity	Represents the concept of positive infinity	1.0 / 0.0, 1e300 / 1e−300, Math.abs (−1.0 / 0.0)
-Infinity	Represents the concept of negative infinity	−1.0 / 0.0, 1.0 / (−0.0), 1e300/−1e−300
-0.0	Represents a negative number close to zero	−1.0 / (1.0 / 0.0), −1e−300 / 1e300
NaN	Represents undefined results	0.0 / 0.0, 1e300 * Float.NaN, Math.sqrt (−9.0)

Positive infinity, negative infinity, and NaN entities are available as double and float constants:

```
Double.POSITIVE_INFINITY; // Infinity
Float.POSITIVE_INFINITY;  // Infinity
Double.NEGATIVE_INFINITY; // -Infinity
Float.NEGATIVE_INFINITY;  // -Infinity
Double.NaN; // Not-a-Number
Float.NaN;  // Not-a-Number
```

The Double and Float wrapper classes have methods to determine if a number is infinite or NaN:

```
Double.isInfinite(Double.POSITIVE_INFINITY); // true
Double.isInfinite(Double.NEGATIVE_INFINITY); // true
Double.isInfinite(1); // false
Double.isNaN(Double.NaN); // true
Double.isNaN(1); // false
Float.isInfinite(Float.POSITIVE_INFINITY); // true
Float.isInfinite(Float.NEGATIVE_INFINITY); // true
Float.isInfinite(1); // false
Float.isNaN(Float.NaN); // true
Float.isNaN(1); // false
```

Operations Involving Special Entities

Table 3-3 shows the results of special entity operations where the operands are abbreviated as INF for Double.POSITIVE_INFINITY, -INF for Double.NEGATIVE_INFINITY, and NAN for Double.NaN.

For example, column 4's heading entry (–0.0) and row 12's entry (* NAN) have a result of NaN, and could be written as follows:

```
// 'NaN' will be printed
System.out.print((-0.0) * Double.NaN);
```

Table 3-3. Operations involving special entities

	INF	(–INF)	(–0.0)
* INF	Infinity	-Infinity	NaN
+ INF	Infinity	NaN	Infinity
– INF	NaN	-Infinity	-Infinity
/ INF	NaN	NaN	-0.0
* 0.0	NaN	NaN	-0.0
+ 0.0	Infinity	-Infinity	0.0
+ 0.5	Infinity	-Infinity	0.5
* 0.5	Infinity	-Infinity	-0.0
+ (–0.5)	Infinity	-Infinity	-0.5
* (–0.5)	-Infinity	Infinity	0.0
+ NAN	NaN	NaN	NaN
* NAN	NaN	NaN	NaN

TIP

Any operation performed on NaN results in NaN; there is no such thing as -NaN.

Numeric Promotion of Primitive Types

Numeric promotion consists of rules that are applied to the operands of an arithmetic operator under certain conditions. Numeric promotion rules consist of both unary and binary promotion rules.

Unary Numeric Promotion

When a primitive of a numeric type is part of an expression, as listed in Table 3-4, the following promotion rules are applied:

- If the operand is of type byte, short, or char, the type will be promoted to type int.

- Otherwise, the type of the operand remains unchanged.

Table 3-4. Expression for unary promotion rules

Expression
Operand of a unary plus operator +
Operand of a unary minus operator −
Operand of a bitwise complement operator ~
All shift operators >>, >>>, or <<
Index expression in an array access expression
Dimension expression in an array creation expression

Binary Numeric Promotion

When two primitives of different numerical types are compared via the operators listed in Table 3-5, one type is promoted based on the following binary promotion rules:

- If either operand is of type double, the non-double primitive is converted to type double.

- If either operand is of type float, the non-float primitive is converted to type float.

- If either operand is of type `long`, the non-`long` primitive is converted to type `long`.

- Otherwise, both operands are converted to `int`.

Table 3-5. Operators for binary promotion rules

Operators	Description
+ and −	Additive operators
*, /, and %	Multiplicative operators
<, <=, >, and >=	Comparison operators
== and !=	Equality operators
&, ^, and |	Bitwise operators
? :	Conditional operator (see next section)

Special Cases for Conditional Operators

- If one operand is of type `byte` and the other is of type `short`, the conditional expression will be of type `short`:

      short = true ? byte : short

- If one operand *R* is of type `byte,` `short`, or `char`, and the other is a constant expression of type `int` whose value is within range of *R*, the conditional expression is of type *R*:

      short = (true ? short : 1967)

- Otherwise, binary numeric promotion is applied and the conditional expression type will be that of the promoted type of the second and third operands.

Wrapper Classes

Each of the primitive types has a corresponding wrapper class/ reference type, which is located in package `java.lang`. Each wrapper class has a variety of methods, including one to return the type's value, as shown in Table 3-6. These integer and floating-point wrapper classes can return values of several primitive types.

Table 3-6. Wrapper classes

Primitive types	Reference types	Methods to get primitive values
boolean	Boolean	booleanValue()
char	Character	charValue()
byte	Byte	byteValue(), shortValue(), intValue(), longValue(), floatValue(), doubleValue()
short	Short	byteValue(), shortValue(), intValue(), longValue(), floatValue(), doubleValue()
int	Integer	byteValue(), shortValue(), intValue(), longValue(), floatValue(), doubleValue()
long	Long	byteValue(), shortValue(), intValue(), longValue(), floatValue(), doubleValue()
float	Float	byteValue(), shortValue(), intValue(), longValue(), floatValue(), doubleValue()
double	Double	byteValue(), shortValue(), intValue(), longValue(), floatValue(), doubleValue()

Autoboxing and Unboxing

Autoboxing and unboxing are typically used for collections of primitives. Autoboxing involves the dynamic allocation of memory and initialization of an object for each primitive. Note that the overhead can often exceed the execution time of the desired operation. Unboxing involves the production of a primitive for each object.

Computationally intensive tasks using primitives (e.g., iterating through primitives in a container) should be done using arrays of primitives in preference to collections of wrapper objects.

Autoboxing

Autoboxing is the automatic conversion of primitive types to their corresponding wrapper classes. In this example, the prize-fighter's weight of 147 is automatically converted to its corresponding wrapper class because collections store references, not primitive values:

```
// Create hash map of weight groups
HashMap<String, Integer> weightGroups
    = new HashMap<String, Integer> ();
weightGroups.put("welterweight", 147);
weightGroups.put("middleweight", 160);
weightGroups.put("cruiserweight", 200);
```

The following example shows an acceptable but not recommended use of autoboxing:

```
// Establish weight allowance
Integer weightAllowanceW = 5; //improper
```

TIP

For these examples, wrapper class variables end with a capital W. This is not the convention.

As there is no reason to force autoboxing, the preceding statement should instead be written as follows:

```
Integer weightAllowanceW = new Integer (5);
```

Unboxing

Unboxing is the automatic conversion of the wrapper classes to their corresponding primitive types. In this example, a reference type is retrieved from the hash map. It is automatically unboxed so that it can fit into the primitive type:

```
// Get the stored weight limit
int weightLimitP = weightGroups.get(middleweight);
```

TIP

For these examples, primitive variables end with a capital P. This is not the convention.

The following example shows an acceptable but not recommended use of unboxing:

```
// Establish the weight allowance
weightLimitP = weightLimitP + weightAllowanceW;
```

It is better to write this expression with the intValue() method, as shown here:

```
weightLimitP = weightLimitP
  + weightAllowanceW.intValue(
);
```

CHAPTER 4

Reference Types

Reference types hold references to objects and provide a means to access those objects stored somewhere in memory. The memory locations are irrelevant to programmers. All reference types are a subclass of type `java.lang.Object`.

Table 4-1 lists the five Java reference types.

Table 4-1. Reference types

Reference type	Brief description
Annotation	Provides a way to associate metadata (data about data) with program elements.
Array	Provides a fixed-size data structure that stores data elements of the same type.
Class	Designed to provide inheritance, polymorphism, and encapsulation. Usually models something in the real world and consists of a set of values that holds data and a set of methods that operates on the data.
Enumeration	A reference for a set of objects that represents a related set of choices.
Interface	Provides a public API and is "implemented" by Java classes.

Comparing Reference Types to Primitive Types

There are two type categories in Java: reference types and primitive types. Table 4-2 shows some of the key comparisons between them. See Chapter 3 for more details.

Table 4-2. Reference types compared to primitive types

Reference types	Primitive types
Unlimited number of reference types, as they are defined by the user.	Consists of `boolean` and numeric types: `char`, `byte`, `short`, `int`, `long`, `float`, and `double`.
Memory location stores a reference to the data.	Memory location stores actual data held by the primitive type.
When a reference type is assigned to another reference type, both will point to the same object.	When a value of a primitive is assigned to another variable of the same type, a copy is made.
When an object is passed into a method, the called method can change the contents of the object passed to it but not the address of the object.	When a primitive is passed into a method, only a copy of the primitive is passed. The called method does not have access to the original primitive value and therefore cannot change it. The called method can change the copied value.

Default Values

Default values are the values assigned to instance variables in Java, when no initialization value has been explicitly set.

Instance and Local Variable Objects

Instance variables (i.e., those declared at the class level) have a default value of `null`. `null` references nothing.

Local variables (i.e., those declared within a method) do not have a default value, not even a value of `null`. Always initialize local variables because they are not given a default value. Checking an uninitialized local variable object for a value (including a value of null) will result in a compile-time error.

Although object references with a value of null do not refer to any object on the heap, objects set to null can be referenced in code *without* receiving compile-time or runtime errors:

```
Date dateOfParty = null;
// This will compile
if (dateOfParty == null) {
    ...
}
```

Invoking a method on a reference variable that is null or using the dot operator on the object will result in a java.lang.Null PointerException:

```
private static int MAX_LENGTH = 20;
...
String theme = null;
// Exception thrown, since theme is null
if (theme.length() > MAX_LENGTH) {
    ...
}
```

Arrays

Arrays are always given a default value whether they are declared as instance variables or local variables. Arrays that are declared but not initialized are given a default value of null.

In the following code, the gameList1 array is initialized but not the individual values, meaning that the object references will have a value of null. Objects have to be added to the array:

```
// The declared arrays named gameList1 and
// gameList2 are initialized to null by default
Game[] gameList1;
Game gameList2[];

// The following array has been initialized but
// the object references are still null since
// the array contains no objects
```

```
    gameList1 = new Game[10];

// Add a Game object to the list
// Now the list has one object
    gameList1[0] = new Game();
```

Multidimensional arrays in Java are actually arrays of arrays. They may be initialized with the new operator or by placing their values within braces. Multidimensional arrays may be uniform or nonuniform in shape:

```
// Anonymous array
int twoDimensionalArray[][] = new int[6][6];
twoDimensionalArray[0][0] = 100;
int threeDimensionalArray[][][] = new int[2][2][2];
threeDimensionalArray[0][0][0] = 200;
int varDimensionArray[][] = {{0,0},{1,1,1},{2,2,2,2}};
varDimensionArray[0][0] = 300;
```

Anonymous arrays allow for the creation of a new array of values anywhere in the code base:

```
// Examples using anonymous arrays
int[] luckyNumbers = new int[] {7, 13, 21};
int totalWinnings = sum(new int[] {3000, 4500, 5000});
```

Conversion of Reference Types

An object can be converted to the type of its superclass (widening) or any of its subclasses (narrowing).

The compiler checks conversions at compile time and the Java Virtual Machine (JVM) checks conversions at runtime.

Widening Conversions

- Widening implicitly converts a subclass to a parent class (superclass).

- Widening conversions do not throw runtime exceptions.

- No explicit cast is necessary:

```
String s = new String();
Object o = s; // widening
```

Narrowing Conversions

- Narrowing converts a more general type into a more specific type.

- Narrowing is a conversion of a superclass to a subclass.

- An explicit cast is required. To cast an object to another object, place the type of object you are casting to in parentheses immediately before the object you are casting.

- Illegitimate narrowing results in a `ClassCastException`.

- Narrowing may result in a loss of data/precision.

Objects cannot be converted to an unrelated type—that is, a type other than one of its subclasses or superclasses. Doing so will generate an `inconvertible types` error at compile time. The following is an example of a conversion that will result in a compile-time error due to `inconvertible types`:

```
Object c = new Object();
String d = (Integer) c;  // compile-time error
```

Converting Between Primitives and Reference Types

The automatic conversion of primitive types to reference types and vice versa is called autoboxing and unboxing, respectively. For more information, refer back to Chapter 3.

Passing Reference Types into Methods

When an object is passed into a method as a variable:

- A copy of the reference variable is passed, not the actual object.

- The caller and the called methods have identical copies of the reference.

- The caller will also see any changes the called method makes to the object. Passing a copy of the object to the called method will prevent it from making changes to the original object.

- The called method cannot change the address of the object, but it can change the contents of the object.

The following example illustrates passing reference types and primitive types into methods and the effects on those types when changed by the called method:

```
void roomSetup() {

  // Reference passing
  Table table = new Table();
    table.setLength(72);
    // Length will be changed
    modTableLength(table);

    // Primitive passing
    // Value of chairs not changed
    int chairs = 8;
    modChairCount(chairs);
  }

  void modTableLength(Table t) {
    t.setLength(36);
  }

  void modChairCount(int i) {
      i = 10;
  }
}
```

Comparing Reference Types

Reference types are comparable in Java. Equality operators and the equals method can be used to assist with comparisons.

Using the Equality Operators

The != and == equality operators are used to compare the memory locations of two objects. If the memory addresses of the objects being compared are the same, the objects are considered equal. These equality operators are not used to compare the contents of two objects.

In the following example, guest1 and guest2 have the same memory address, so the statement "They are equal" will be output:

```
Guest guest1 = new Guest("name");
Guest guest2 = guest1;
if (guest1 == guest2)
  System.out.println("They are equal")
```

In the following example, the memory addresses are not equal, so the statement "They are not equal" will be output:

```
Guest guest3 = new Guest("name");
Guest guest4 = new Guest("name");
if (guest3 == guest4)
  System.out.println("They are equal.")
else
  System.out.println("They are not equal")
```

Using the equals() Method

To compare the contents of two class objects, the equals()method from class Object can be used or overridden. When the equals() method is overridden, the hashCode()method should also be overridden. This is done for compatibility with hash-based collections such as HashMap() and HashSet().

For example, if you want to compare values contained in two instances of the same class, you should use a programmer-defined equals() method.

Comparing Strings

There are two ways to check whether strings are equal in Java, but the definition of "equal" for each of them is different. Typically, if the goal is to compare character sequences contained in two strings, the equals() method should be used:

- The equals() method compares two strings, character by character, to determine equality. This is not the default implementation of the equals() method provided by the Object class. This is the overridden implementation provided by String class.

- The == operator checks to see whether two object references refer to the same instance of an object.

Here is a program that shows how strings are evaluated using the equals() method and the == operator (for more information on how strings are evaluated, see "String Literals" on page 15 in Chapter 2):

```
class MyComparisons {

    // Add string to pool
    String first = "chairs";
    // Use string from pool
    String second = "chairs";
    // Create a new string
    String third = new String ("chairs");
```

```java
void myMethod() {

  // Contrary to popular belief, this evaluates
  // to true. Try it!
  if (first == second) {
    System.out.println("first == second");
  }

  // This evaluates to true
  if (first.equals(second)) {
    System.out.println("first equals second");
  }
  // This evaluates to false
  if (first == third) {
    System.out.println("first == third");
  }
  // This evaluates to true
  if (first.equals(third)) {
    System.out.println("first equals third");
  }
} // End myMethod()
} //end class
```

TIP

Objects of the String class are immutable. Objects of the
StringBuffer and StringBuilder classes are mutable.

Comparing Enumerations

enum values can be compared using == or the equals()method,
as they return the same result. The == operator is used more
frequently to compare enumeration types.

Copying Reference Types

When reference types are copied, either a copy of the reference to an object is made, or an actual copy of the object is made, creating a new object. The latter is referred to as *cloning* in Java.

Copying a Reference to an Object

When copying a reference to an object, the result is one object with two references. In the following example, closingSong is assigned a reference to the object pointed to by lastSong. Any changes made to lastSong will be reflected in closingSong and vice versa:

```
Song lastSong = new Song();
Song closingSong = lastSong;
```

Cloning Objects

Cloning results in another copy of the object, not just a copy of a reference to an object. Cloning is not available to classes by default. Note that cloning is usually very complex, so you should consider a copy constructor instead:

- For a class to be cloneable, it must implement the interface Cloneable.

- The protected method clone() allows for objects to clone themselves.

- For an object to clone an object other than itself, the clone() method must be overridden and made public by the object being cloned.

- When cloning, a cast must be used because clone() returns type object.

- Cloning can throw a CloneNotSupportedException.

Shallow and deep cloning

Shallow and deep cloning are the two types of cloning in Java.

In shallow cloning, primitive values and the references in the object being cloned are copied. Copies of the objects referred to by those references are not made.

In the following example, leadingSong will be assigned the values in length and year, as they are primitive types, and references to title and artist, as they are reference types:

```
Class Song {
  String title;
  Artist artist;
  float length;
  int year;
  void setData() {...}
}
Song firstSong = new Song();
try {
  // Make an actual copy by cloning
  Song leadingSong = (Song)firstSong.clone();
} catch (CloneNotSupportedException cnse)
  cnse.printStackTrace();
} // end
```

In deep cloning, the cloned object makes a copy of each of its object's fields, recursing through all other objects referenced by it. A deep-clone method must be defined by the programmer, as the Java API does not provide one. Alternatives to deep cloning are serialization and copy constructors. (Copy constructors are often preferred over serialization.)

Memory Allocation and Garbage Collection of Reference Types

When a new object is created, memory is allocated. When there are no references to an object, the memory that object used can be reclaimed during the garbage collection process. For more information on this topic, see Chapter 11.

CHAPTER 5

Object-Oriented Programming

Basic elements of object-oriented programming (OOP) in Java include classes, objects, and interfaces.

Classes and Objects

Classes define entities that usually represent something in the real world. They consist of a set of values that holds data and a set of methods that operates on the data.

An instance of a class is called an *object*, and it is allocated memory. There can be multiple instances of a class.

Classes can inherit data members and methods from other classes. A class can directly inherit from only one class—the *superclass*. A class can have only one direct superclass. This is called *inheritance*.

When implementing a class, the inner details of the class should be private and accessible only through public interfaces. This is called *encapsulation*. The JavaBean convention is to use accessor and mutator methods (e.g., getFirstName() and setFirst Name("Leonardina")) to indirectly access the private members of a class and to ensure that another class cannot unexpectedly modify private members. Returning immutable values (i.e., strings, primitive values, and objects intentionally made immutable) is another way to protect the data members from being altered by other objects.

Class Syntax

A class has a class signature, optional constructors, data members, and methods:

```
[javaModifiers] class className
  [extends someSuperClass]
  [implements someInterfaces separated by commas] {
  // Data member(s)
  // Constructor(s)
  // Method(s)
}
```

Instantiating a Class (Creating an Object)

An object is an instance of a class. Once instantiated, objects have their own set of data members and methods:

```
// Sample class definitions
public class Candidate {...}
class Stats extends ToolSet {...}


public class Report extends ToolSet
  implements Runnable {...}
```

Separate objects of class Candidate are created (instantiated) using the keyword new:

```
Candidate candidate1 = new Candidate();
Candidate candidate2 = new Candidate();
```

Data Members and Methods

Data members, also known as fields, hold data about a class. Data members that are nonstatic are also called instance variables:

```
[javaModifier] type dataMemberName
```

Methods operate on class data:

```
[javaModifiers] type methodName (parameterList)
[throws listOfExceptionsSeparatedByCommas]  {
  // Method body
}
```

The following is an example of class Candidate and its data members and methods:

```
public class Candidate {
  // Data members or fields
  private String firstName;
  private String lastName;
  private int year;
  // Methods
  public void setYear  (int y) { year = y; }
  public String getLastName() {return lastName;}
} // End class Candidate
```

Accessing Data Members and Methods in Objects

The dot operator (.) is used to access data members and methods in objects. It is not necessary to use the dot operator when accessing data members or methods from within an object:

```
candidate1.setYear(2016);
String name = getFirstName() + getLastName();
```

Overloading

Methods including constructors can be overloaded. Overloading means that two or more methods have the same name but different signatures (parameters and return values). Note that overloaded methods must have different parameters, and they may have different return types; but having only different return types is not overloading. The access modifiers of overloaded methods can be different:

```
public class VotingMachine {
  ...
  public void startUp() {...}
  private void startUp(int delay) {...}
}
```

When a method is overloaded, it is permissible for each of its signatures to throw different checked exceptions:

```
private String startUp(District d) throws new
IOException {...}
```

Overriding

A subclass can override the methods it inherits. When overridden, a method contains the same signature (name and parameters) as a method in its superclass, but it has different implementation details.

The method startUp() in superclass Display is overridden in class TouchScreenDisplay:

```
public class Display {
  void startUp(){
    System.out.println("Using base display.");
  }
}
public class TouchScreenDisplay extends Display {
    void startUp() {
    System.out.println("Using new display.");
  }
}
```

Rules regarding overriding methods include the following:

- Methods that are not final, private, or static can be overridden.

- Protected methods can override methods that do not have access modifiers.

- The overriding method cannot have a more restrictive access modifier (i.e., package, public, private, protected) than the original method.

- The overriding method cannot throw any new checked exceptions.

Constructors

Constructors are called upon object creation and are used to initialize data in the newly created object. Constructors are optional, have exactly the same name as the class, and they do not have a return in the body (as methods do).

A class can have multiple constructors. The constructor that is called when a new object is created is the one that has a matching signature:

```java
public class Candidate {
  ...
  Candidate(int id) {
    this.identification = id;
  }
  Candidate(int id, int age) {
    this.identification = id;
    this.age = age;
  }
}
// Create a new Candidate and call its constructor
class ElectionManager   {
  int i = getIdFromConsole();
  Candidate candidate = new Candidate();
}
```

Classes implicitly have a no-argument constructor if no explicit constructor is present. Note that if a constructor with arguments is added, there will be no no-argument constructor unless it is manually added.

Superclasses and Subclasses

In Java, a class (known as the *subclass*) can inherit directly from one class (known as the *superclass*). The Java keyword extends indicates that a class inherits data members and methods from another class. Subclasses do not have direct access to private members of its superclass, but do have access to the public and protected members of the superclass. A subclass also has access to members of the superclass where the same package is shared (*package-private* or `protected`). As previously mentioned, accessor and mutator methods provide a mechanism to indirectly access the `private` members of a class, including a superclass:

```
public class Machine {
  boolean state;
  void setState(boolean s) {state = s;}
  boolean getState() {return state;}
}
public class VotingMachine extends Machine {
  ...
}
```

The keyword `super` in the `Curtain` class's default constructor is used to access methods in the superclass overridden by methods in the subclass:

```
public class PrivacyWall {
  public void printSpecs() {...}

}
public class Curtain extends PrivacyWall {
  public void printSpecs() {
    ...
    super.printSpecs();
  }
}
```

Another common use of the keyword `super` is to call the constructor of a superclass and pass it parameters. Note that this call must be the first statement in the constructor calling super:

```
public PrivacyWall(int l, int w) {
  int length = l;
  int width = w;
}

public class Curtain extends PrivacyWall {
  // Set default length and width
  public Curtain() {super(15, 25);}
}
```

If there is not an explicit call to the constructor of the superclass, an automatic call to the no-argument constructor of the superclass is made.

The this Keyword

The three common uses of the this keyword are to refer to the current object, to call a constructor from within another constructor in the same class, and to pass a reference of the current object to another object.

To assign a parameter variable to an instance variable of the current object:

```
public class Curtain extends PrivacyWall {
  String color;
  public setColor(String color) {
    this.color = color;
  }
}
```

To call a constructor from another constructor in the same class:

```
public class Curtain extends PrivacyWall {
  public Curtain(int length, int width) {}
  public Curtain() {this(10, 9);}
}
```

To pass a reference of the current object to another object:

```
public class Curtain {
  Builder builder = new Builder();
  builder.setWallType(this);
}

public class Builder {
  public void setWallType(Curtain c) {...}
}
```

Variable-Length Argument Lists

Since Java 5.0, methods can have a variable-length argument list. Called *varargs*, these methods are declared such that the last (and only the last) argument can be repeated zero or more times when the method is called. The vararg parameter can be either a primitive or an object. An ellipsis (...) is used in the argument list of the method signature to declare the method as a vararg. The syntax of the vararg parameter is as follows:

```
type... objectOrPrimitiveName
```

Here is an example of a signature for a vararg method:

```
public setDisplayButtons(int row,
  String... names) {...}
```

The Java compiler modifies vararg methods to look like regular methods. The previous example would be modified at compile time to:

```
public setDisplayButtons(int row,
  String [] names) {...}
```

It is permissible for a vararg method to have a vararg parameter as its only parameter:

```
// Zero or more rows
public void setDisplayButtons (String... names) {...}
```

A vararg method is called the same way an ordinary method is called except that it can take a variable number of parameters, repeating only the last argument:

```
setDisplayButtons("Jim");
setDisplayButtons("John", "Mary", "Pete");
setDisplayButtons("Sue", "Doug", "Terry", "John");
```

The printf method is often used when formatting a variable set of output, as printf is a vararg method. From the Java API, type the following:

```
public PrintStream printf(String format,
  Object... args)
```

The printf method is called with a format string and a variable set of objects:

```
System.out.printf("Hello voter %s%n
  This is machine %d%n", "Sally", 1);
```

For detailed information on formatting a string passed into the `printf` method, see `java.util.Formatter`.

The enhanced `for` loop (for each) is often used to iterate through the variable argument:

```
printRows() {
  for (String name: names)
    System.out.println(name);
}
```

Abstract Classes and Abstract Methods

Abstract classes and methods are declared with the keyword `abstract`.

Abstract Classes

An abstract class is typically used as a base class and cannot be instantiated. It can contain abstract and nonabstract methods, and it can be a subclass of an abstract or a nonabstract class. All of its abstract methods must be defined by the classes that inherit (extend) it unless the subclass is also abstract:

```
public abstract class Alarm {
  public void reset() {...}
  public abstract void renderAlarm();
}
```

Abstract Methods

An abstract method contains only the method declaration, which must be defined by any nonabstract class that inherits it:

```
public class DisplayAlarm extends Alarm {
  public void renderAlarm() {
    System.out.println("Active alarm.");
  }
}
```

Static Data Members, Static Methods, Static Constants, and Static Initializers

Static data members, methods, constants, and initializers reside with a class and not instances of classes. Static data members, methods, and constants can be accessed in the class they are defined in or in another class using the dot operator.

Static Data Members

Static data members have the same features as static methods, plus they are stored in a single location in memory.

They are used when only one copy of a data member is needed across all instances of a class (e.g., a counter):

```
// Declaring a static data member
public class Voter  {
  static int voterCount = 0;
  public Voter() { voterCount++;}
  public static int getVoterCount() {
    return voterCount;
  }
}
...
int numVoters = Voter.voterCount;
```

Static Methods

Static methods have the keyword static in the method declaration:

```
// Declaring a static method
class Analyzer {
  public static int getVotesByAge() {...}
}
// Using the static method
Analyzer.getVotesByAge();
```

Static methods cannot access nonstatic methods or variables because static methods are associated with a class, not an object.

Static Constants

Static constants are static members declared constant. They have the keywords `static` and `final`, and a program cannot change them:

```
// Declaring a static constant
static final int AGE_LIMIT = 18;
// Using a static constant
if (age == AGE_LIMIT)
  newVoter = "yes";
```

Static Initializers

Static initializers include a block of code prefaced by the keyword `static`. A class can have any number of static initializer blocks, and it is guaranteed that they will run in the order in which they appear. Static initializer blocks are executed only once per class initialization:

```
// Static Initializer
static {
  numberOfCandidates = getNumberOfCandidates();
}
```

Interfaces

Interfaces provide a set of declared `public` methods that do not have method bodies. A class that implements an interface must provide concrete implementations of all the methods defined by the interface, or it must be declared abstract.

An interface is declared using the keyword `interface`, followed by the name of the interface and a set of method declarations.

Interface names are usually adjectives and end with "able" or "ible," as the interface provides a capability:

```
interface Reportable  {
  void genReport(String repType);
  void printReport(String repType);
}
```

A class that implements an interface must indicate so in its class signature with the keyword implements:

```
class VotingMachine implements Reportable {
  public void genReport (String repType) {
    Report report = new Report(repType);
  }
  public void printReport(String repType) {
    System.out.println(repType);
  }
}
```

TIP

Classes can implement multiple interfaces, and interfaces can extend multiple interfaces.

Enumerations

In simplest terms, enumerations are a set of objects that represent a related set of choices:

```
enum DisplayButton {ROUND, SQUARE}
DisplayButton round = DisplayButton.ROUND;
```

Looking beyond simplest terms, an enumeration is a class of type enum. Enum classes can have methods, constructors, and data members:

```
enum DisplayButton {
    // Size in inches
    ROUND (.50),
    SQUARE (.40);
    private final float size;
    DisplayButton(float size) {this.size = size;}
    private float size()  { return size; }
}
```

The method values() returns an array of the ordered list of objects defined for the enum:

```
for (DisplayButton b : DisplayButton.values())
  System.out.println("Button: " + b.size());
```

Annotation Types

Annotations provide a way to associate metadata (data about data) with program elements at compile time and runtime. Packages, classes, methods, fields, parameters, variables, and constructors can be annotated.

Built-in Annotations

Java annotations provide a way to obtain metadata about a class. Java has three built-in annotation types, as depicted in Table 5-1. These annotation types are contained in the `java.lang` package.

Annotations must be placed directly before the item being annotated. They do not have any parameters and do not throw exceptions. Annotations return primitive types, enumerations, class `String`, class `Class`, annotations, and arrays (of these types).

Table 5-1. Built-in annotations

Annotation type	Description
@Override	Indicates that the method is intended to override a method in a superclass.
@Deprecated	Indicates that a deprecated API is being used or overridden.
@SuppressWarnings	Used to selectively suppress warnings.

The following is an example of their use:

```
@Override
  public String toString() {
    return super.toString() + " more";
  }
```

Because `@Override` is a marker annotation, a compile warning will be returned if the method to be overridden cannot be found.

Developer-Defined Annotations

Developers can define their own annotations using three annotation types. A *marker* annotation has no parameters, a *single value* annotation has a single parameter, and a *multivalue* annotation has multiple parameters.

The definition of an annotation is the symbol @, followed by the word `interface`, followed by the name of the annotation.

The meta-annotation `Retention` indicates that an annotation should be retained by the VM so that it can be read at runtime. `Retention` is in the package `java.lang.annotation`:

```
@Retention(RetentionPolicy.RUNTIME)
public @interface Feedback {} // Marker
public @interface Feedback {
  String reportName();
} // Single value
public @interface Feedback {
  String reportName();
  String comment() default "None";
} // Multi value
```

Place the user-defined annotation directly before the item being annotated:

```
@Feedback(reportName="Report 1")
public void myMethod() {...}
```

Programs can check the existence of annotations and obtain annotation values by calling `getAnnotation()` on a method:

```
Feedback fb =
  myMethod.getAnnotation(Feedback.class);
```

CHAPTER 6

Statements and Blocks

A statement is a single command that performs some activity when executed by the Java interpreter:

```
GigSim simulator = new GigSim("Let's play guitar!");
```

Java statements include expression, empty, block, conditional, iteration, transfer of control, exception handling, variable, labeled, assert, and synchronized statements.

Reserved Java words used in statements are `if`, `else`, `switch`, `case`, `while`, `do`, `for`, `break`, `continue`, `return`, `synchronized`, `throw`, `try`, `catch`, `finally`, and `assert`.

Expression Statements

An expression statement is a statement that changes the program state; it is a Java expression that ends in a semicolon. Expression statements include assignments, prefix and postfix increments, prefix and postfix decrements, object creation, and method calls. The following are examples of expression statements:

```
isWithinOperatingHours = true;
++fret; patron++; --glassOfWater; pick--;
Guitarist guitarist = new Guitarist();
guitarist.placeCapo(guitar, capo, fret);
```

Empty Statement

The empty statement provides no additional functionality and is written as a single semicolon (;) or as an empty block {}.

Blocks

A group of statements is called a block or statement block. A block of statements is enclosed in braces. Variables and classes declared in the block are called local variables and local classes, respectively. The scope of local variables and classes is the block in which they are declared.

In blocks, one statement is interpreted at a time in the order in which it was written or in the order of flow control. The following is an example of a block:

```
static {
  GigSimProperties.setFirstFestivalActive(true);
  System.out.println("First festival has begun");
  gigsimLogger.info("Simulator started 1st festival");
}
```

Conditional Statements

if, if else, and if else if are decision-making control flow statements. They are used to execute statements conditionally. The expression for any of these statements must have type Boolean or boolean. Type Boolean is subject to unboxing, auto-conversion of Boolean to boolean.

The if Statement

The if statement consists of an expression and a statement or a block of statements that are executed if the expression evaluates to true:

```
Guitar guitar = new Guitar();
guitar.addProblemItem("Whammy bar");
if (guitar.isBroken()) {
```

```
   Luthier luthier = new Luthier();
   luthier.repairGuitar(guitar);
}
```

The if else Statement

When using else with if, the first block of statements is executed
if the expression evaluates to true; otherwise, the block of code
in the else is executed:

```
CoffeeShop coffeeshop = new CoffeeShop();
if (coffeeshop.getPatronCount() > 5) {
   System.out.println("Play the event.");
} else {
   System.out.println("Go home without pay.");
}
```

The if else if Statement

if else if is typically used when you need to choose among
multiple blocks of code. When the criteria are not met to execute
any of the blocks, the block of code in the final else is executed:

```
ArrayList<Song> playList = new ArrayList<>();
Song song1 = new Song("Mister Sandman");
Song song2 = new Song("Amazing Grace");
playList.add(song1);
playList.add(song2);
...
int numOfSongs = playList.size();
if (numOfSongs <= 24) {
   System.out.println("Do not book");
} else if ((numOfSongs > 24) & (numOfSongs < 50)){
   System.out.println("Book for one night");
} else if ((numOfSongs >= 50)) {
   System.out.println("Book for two nights");
} else {
   System.out.println("Book for the week");
}
```

The switch Statement

The switch statement is a control flow statement that starts with an expression and transfers control to one of the case statements based on the value of the expression. A switch works with char, byte, short, int, as well as Character, Byte, Short, and Integer wrapper types; enumeration types; and the String type. Support for String objects was added in Java SE 7. The break statement is used to exit out of a switch statement. If a case statement does not contain a break, the line of code after the completion of the case will be executed.

This continues until either a break statement is reached or the end of the switch is reached. One default label is permitted and is often listed last for readability:

```
String style;
String guitarist = "Eric Clapton";
...
switch (guitarist) {
  case "Chet Atkins":
    style = "Nashville sound";
    break;
  case "Thomas Emmanuel":
    style = "Complex fingerstyle";
    break;
  default:
    style = "Unknown";
    break;
}
```

Iteration Statements

The for loop, enhanced for loop, while, and do-while statements are iteration statements. They are used for iterating through pieces of code.

The for Loop

The for statement contains three parts: initialization, expression, and update. As shown next, the variable (i.e., i) in the statement must be initialized before being used. The expression (i.e., i<bArray.length()) is evaluated before iterating through the loop (i.e., i++). The iteration takes place only if the expression is true and the variable is updated after each iteration:

```java
Banjo [] bArray = new Banjo[2];
bArray[0] = new Banjo();
bArray[0].setManufacturer("Windsor");
bArray[1] = new Banjo();
bArray[1].setManufacturer("Gibson");
for (int i=0; i<bArray.length; i++){
   System.out.println(bArray[i].getManufacturer());
}
```

The Enhanced for Loop

The enhanced for loop, a.k.a. the "for in" loop and "for each" loop, is used for iteration through an iterable object or array. The loop is executed once for each element of the array or collection and does not use a counter, as the number of iterations is already determined:

```java
ElectricGuitar eGuitar1 = new ElectricGuitar();
eGuitar1.setName("Blackie");
ElectricGuitar eGuitar2 = new ElectricGuitar();
eGuitar2.setName("Lucille");
ArrayList <ElectricGuitar> eList = new ArrayList<>();
eList.add(eGuitar1); eList.add(eGuitar2);
for (ElectricGuitar e : eList) {
   System.out.println("Name:" + e.getName());
}
```

The while Loop

In a while statement, the expression is evaluated and the loop is executed only if the expression evaluates to true. The expression can be of type boolean or Boolean:

```java
int bandMembers = 5;
while (bandMembers > 3) {
   CoffeeShop c = new CoffeeShop();
   c.performGig(bandMembers);
```

```
    Random generator = new Random();
    bandMembers = generator.nextInt(7) + 1; // 1-7
}
```

The do while Loop

In a do while statement, the loop is always executed at least once
and will continue to be executed as long as the expression is
true. The expression can be of type boolean or Boolean:

```
int bandMembers = 1;
do {
  CoffeeShop c = new CoffeeShop();
  c.performGig(bandMembers);
  Random generator = new Random();
  bandMembers = generator.nextInt(7) + 1; // 1-7
} while (bandMembers > 3);
```

Transfer of Control

Transfer of control statements are used to change the flow of
control in a program. These include the break, continue, and
return statements.

The break Statement

An unlabeled break statement is used to exit the body of a switch
statement or to immediately exit the loop in which it is contained.
Loop bodies include those for the for loop, enhanced for loop,
while, and do-while iteration statements:

```
Song song = new Song("Pink Panther");
Guitar guitar = new Guitar();
int measure = 1; int lastMeasure = 10;
while (measure <= lastMeasure) {
  if (guitar.checkForBrokenStrings()) {
    break;
  }
  song.playMeasure(measure);
  measure++;
}
```

A labeled break forces a break of the loop statement immediately following the label. Labels are typically used with for and while loops when there are nested loops and there is a need to identify which loop to break. To label a loop or a statement, place the label statement immediately before the loop or statement being labeled, as follows:

```
...
playMeasures:
while (isWithinOperatingHours()) {
  while (measure <= lastMeasure) {
    if (guitar.checkForBrokenStrings()) {
      break playMeasures;
    }
    song.playMeasure(measure);
    measure++;
  }
} // exits to here
```

The continue Statement

When executed, the unlabeled continue statement stops the execution of the current for loop, enhanced for loop, while, or do-while statements and starts the next iteration of the loop. The rules for testing loop conditions apply. A labeled continue statement forces the next iteration of the loop statement immediately following the label:

```
for (int i=0; i<25; i++) {
  if (playList.get(i).isPlayed()) {
    continue;
  } else {
    song.playAllMeasures();
  }
}
```

The return Statement

The return statement is used to exit a method and return a value if the method specifies to return a value:

```
private int numberOfFrets = 18; // default
...
public int getNumberOfFrets() {
  return numberOfFrets;
}
```

The return statement will be optional when it is the last statement in a method and the method doesn't return anything.

Synchronized Statement

The Java keyword synchronized can be used to limit access to sections of code (i.e., entire methods) to a single thread. It provides the capability to control access to resources shared by multiple threads. See Chapter 14 for more information.

Assert Statement

Assertions are Boolean expressions used to check whether code behaves as expected while running in debug mode (i.e., using the -enableassertions or -ea switch with the Java interpreter). Assertions are written as follows:

```
assert boolean_expression;
```

Assertions help identify bugs more easily, including identifying unexpected values. They are designed to validate assumptions that should always be true. While running in debug mode, if the assertion evaluates to false, a java.lang.AssertionError is thrown and the program exits; otherwise, nothing happens. Assertions need to be explicitly enabled. To find command-line arguments used to enable assertions, see Chapter 10.

```
// 'strings' value should be 4, 5, 6, 7, 8 or 12
assert (strings == 12 ||
  (strings >= 4 & strings <= 8));
```

Assertions may also be written to include an optional error code. Although called an error code, it is really just text or a value to be used for informational purposes only.

When an assertion that contains an error code evaluates to false, the error code value is turned into a string and displayed to the user immediately prior to the program exiting:

```
assert boolean_expression : errorcode;
```

An example of an assertion using an error code is as follows:

```
// Show invalid 'stringed instruments' strings value
assert (strings == 12 ||
  (strings >= 4 & strings <= 8))
  : "Invalid string count: " + strings;
```

Exception Handling Statements

Exception handling statements are used to specify code to be executed during unusual circumstances. The keywords throw and try/catch/finally are used for exception handling. For more information on exception handling, see Chapter 7.

CHAPTER 7

Exception Handling

An *exception* is an anomalous condition that alters or interrupts the flow of execution. Java provides built-in exception handling to deal with such conditions. Exception handling should not be part of normal program flow.

The Exception Hierarchy

As shown in Figure 7-1, all exceptions and errors inherit from the class Throwable, which inherits from the class Object.

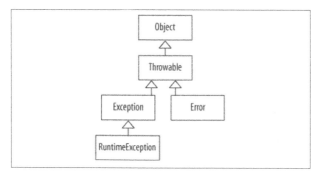

Figure 7-1. Snapshot of the exception hierarchy

Checked/Unchecked Exceptions and Errors

Exceptions and errors fall into three categories: checked exceptions, unchecked exceptions, and errors.

Checked Exceptions

- Checked exceptions are checked by the compiler at compile time.

- Methods that throw a checked exception must indicate so in the method declaration using the throws clause. This must continue all the way up the calling stack until the exception is handled.

- All checked exceptions must be explicitly caught with a catch block.

- Checked exceptions include exceptions of the type Exception, and all classes that are subtypes of Exception, except for RuntimeException and the subtypes of RuntimeException.

The following is an example of a method that throws a checked exception:

```
// Method declaration that throws
// an IOException
void readFile(String filename)
  throws IOException {
  ...
}
```

Unchecked Exceptions

- The compiler does not check unchecked exceptions at compile time.

- Unchecked exceptions occur during runtime due to programmer error (out-of-bounds index, divide by zero, and null pointer exception) or system resource exhaustion.

- Unchecked exceptions do not have to be caught.

- Methods that may throw an unchecked exception do not have to (but can) indicate this in the method declaration.

- Unchecked exceptions include exceptions of the type Run timeException and all subtypes of RuntimeException.

Errors

- Errors are typically unrecoverable and present serious conditions.

- Errors are not checked at compile time and do not have to be (but can be) caught/handled.

TIP

Any checked exceptions, unchecked exceptions, or errors can be caught.

Common Checked/Unchecked Exceptions and Errors

There are various checked exceptions, unchecked exceptions, and unchecked errors that are part of the standard Java platform. Some are more likely to occur than others.

Common Checked Exceptions

ClassNotFoundException
> Thrown when a class cannot be loaded because its definition cannot be found.

`IOException`
> Thrown when a failed or interrupted operation occurs. Two common subtypes of `IOException` are `EOFException` and `FileNotFoundException`.

`FileNotFoundException`
> Thrown when an attempt is made to open a file that cannot be found.

`SQLException`
> Thrown when there is a database error.

`InterruptedException`
> Thrown when a thread is interrupted.

`NoSuchMethodException`
> Thrown when a called method cannot be found.

`CloneNotSupportedException`
> Thrown when `clone()` is called by an object that is not cloneable.

Common Unchecked Exceptions

`ArithmeticException`
> Thrown to indicate that an exceptional arithmetic condition has occurred.

`ArrayIndexOutOfBoundsException`
> Thrown to indicate index out of range.

`ClassCastException`
> Thrown to indicate an attempt to cast an object to a subclass of which it is not an instance.

`IllegalArgumentException`
> Thrown to indicate that an invalid argument has been passed to a method.

`IllegalStateException`
> Thrown to indicate that a method has been called at an inappropriate time.

`IndexOutOfBoundsException`
> Thrown to indicate that an index is out of range.

`NullPointerException`
> Thrown when code references a null object but a nonnull object is required.

`NumberFormatException`
> Thrown to indicate an invalid attempt to convert a string to a numeric type.

Common Errors

`AssertionError`
> Thrown to indicate that an assertion failed.

`ExceptionInInitializeError`
> Thrown to indicate an unexpected exception in a static initializer.

`VirtualMachineError`
> Thrown to indicate a problem with the JVM.

`OutOfMemoryError`
> Thrown when there is no more memory available to allocate an object or perform garbage collection.

`NoClassDefFoundError`
> Thrown when the JVM cannot find a class definition that was found at compile time.

`StackOverflowError`
> Thrown to indicate that a stack overflow occurs.

Exception Handling Keywords

In Java, error-handling code is cleanly separated from error-generating code. Code that generates the exception is said to "throw" an exception, whereas code that handles the exception is said to "catch" the exception:

```
// Declare an exception
public void methodA() throws IOException {
  ...
  throw new IOException();
  ...
}

// Catch an exception
public void methodB() {
  ...
  /* Call to methodA must be in a try/catch block
  ** since the exception is a checked exception;
  ** otherwise methodB could throw the exception */
  try {
      methodA();

  }catch (IOException ioe) {
    System.err.println(ioe.getMessage());
    ioe.printStackTrace();
  }
}
```

The throw Keyword

To throw an exception, use the keyword throw. Any checked/unchecked exception and error can be thrown:

```
if (n == -1)
   throw new EOFException();
```

The try/catch/finally Keywords

Thrown exceptions are handled by a Java try, catch, finally block. The Java interpreter looks for code to handle the exception, first looking in the enclosed block of code, and then propagating up the call stack to main() if necessary. If the exception is not handled, the program exits and a stack trace is printed:

```
try {
  method();
} catch (EOFException eofe) {
  eofe.printStackTrace();
```

```
} catch (IOException ioe) {
  ioe.printStackTrace();
} finally {
  // cleanup
}
```

The try-catch Statement

The try-catch statement includes one try and one or more catch blocks.

The try block contains code that may throw exceptions. All checked exceptions that may be thrown must have a catch block to handle the exception. If no exceptions are thrown, the try block terminates normally. A try block may have zero or more catch clauses to handle the exceptions.

TIP

A try block must have at least one catch or finally block associated with it.

There cannot be any code between the try block and any of the catch blocks (if present) or the finally block (if present).

The catch block(s) contain code to handle thrown exceptions, including printing information about the exception to a file, giving users an opportunity to input correct information. Note that catch blocks should never be empty because such "silencing" results in exceptions being hidden, making errors harder to debug.

A common convention for naming the parameter in the catch clause is a set of letters representing each of the words in the name of the exception:

```
catch (ArrayIndexOutOfBoundsException aioobe) {
  aioobe.printStackStrace();
}
```

Within a catch clause, a new exception may also be thrown if necessary.

The order of the catch clauses in a try/catch block defines the precedence for catching exceptions. Always begin with the most specific exception that may be thrown and end with the most general.

TIP

Exceptions thrown in the try block are directed to the first catch clause containing arguments of the same type as the exception object or superclass of that type. The catch block with the Exception parameter should always be last in the ordered list.

If none of the parameters for the catch clauses match the exception thrown, the system will search for the parameter that matches the superclass of the exception.

The try-finally Statement

The try-finally statement includes one try and one finally block.

The finally block is used for releasing resources when necessary:

```
public void testMethod() throws IOException {
FileWriter fileWriter =
  new FileWriter("\\data.txt");
  try {
    fileWriter.write("Information...");
  } finally {
    fileWriter.close();
  }
}
```

This block is optional and is only used where needed. When used, it is executed last in a try-finally block and will always be executed, whether or not the try block terminates normally. If the finally block throws an exception, it must be handled.

The try-catch-finally Statement

The try-catch-finally statement includes one try, one or more catch blocks, and one finally block.

For this statement, the finally block is also used for cleanup and releasing resources:

```java
public void testMethod() {
  FileWriter fileWriter = null;
  try {
    fileWriter = new FileWriter("\\data.txt");
    fileWriter.write("Information...");
  } catch (IOException ex) {
    ex.printStackTrace();
  } finally {
    try {
      fileWriter.close();
    } catch (Exception e) {
      e.printStackTrace();
    }
  }
}
```

This block is optional and is only used where needed. When used, it is executed last in a try-catch-finally block and will always be executed, whether or not the try block terminates normally or the catch clause(s) were executed. If the finally block throws an exception, it must be handled.

The try-with-resources Statement

The try-with-resources statement is used for declaring resources that must be closed when they are no longer needed. These resources are declared in the try block:

```java
public void testMethod() throws IOException {
  try (FileWriter fw = new FileWriter("\\data.txt"))
  {
     fw.write("Information...");
  }
}
```

Any resource that implements the Autoclosable interface may be used with the try-with-resources statement.

The multi-catch Clause

The multi-catch clause is used to allow for multiple exception arguments in one catch clause:

```java
boolean isTest = false;
public void testMethod() {
  try {
    if (isTest) {
      throw new IOException();
    } else {
      throw new SQLException();
    }
  } catch (IOException | SQLException e) {
    e.printStackTrace();
  }
}
```

The Exception Handling Process

Here are the steps to the exception handling process:

1. An exception is encountered resulting in an exception object being created.

2. A new exception object is thrown.

3. The runtime system looks for code to handle the exception beginning with the method in which the exception object was created. If no handler is found, the runtime environment traverses the call stack (the ordered list of methods) in reverse looking for an exception handler. If the exception

is not handled, the program exits and a stack trace is automatically output.

4. The runtime system hands the exception object off to an exception handler to handle (catch) the exception.

Defining Your Own Exception Class

Programmer-defined exceptions should be created when those other than the existing Java exceptions are necessary. In general, the Java exceptions should be reused wherever possible:

- To define a checked exception, the new exception class must extend the Exception class, directly or indirectly.

- To define an unchecked exception, the new exception class must extend the RuntimeException class, directly or indirectly.

- To define an unchecked error, the new error class must extend the Error class.

User-defined exceptions should have at least two constructors—a constructor that does not accept any arguments and a constructor that does:

```
public class ReportException extends Exception {
  public ReportException () {}
  public ReportException (String message, int
    reportId) {
    ...
  }
}
```

Printing Information About Exceptions

The methods in the Throwable class that provide information about thrown exceptions are getMessage(), toString, and print StackTrace(). In general, one of these methods should be called in the catch clause handling the exception. Programmers can also write code to obtain additional useful information when an exception occurs (i.e., the name of the file that was not found).

The getMessage() Method

The getMessage() method returns a detailed message string about the exception:

```
try {
  new FileReader("file.js");
} catch (FileNotFoundException fnfe) {
  System.err.println(fnfe.getMessage());
}
```

The toString() Method

This toString() method returns a detailed message string about the exception, including its class name:

```
try {
  new FileReader("file.js");
} catch (FileNotFoundException fnfe) {
    System.err.println(fnfe.toString());
}
```

The printStackTrace() Method

This printStackTrace() method returns a detailed message string about the exception, including its class name and a stack trace from where the error was caught, all the way back to where it was thrown:

```
try {
  new FileReader("file.js");
} catch (FileNotFoundException fnfe) {
  fnfe.printStackTrace();
}
```

The following is an example of a stack trace. The first line contains the contents returned when the toString() method is invoked on an exception object. The remainder shows the method calls beginning with the location where the exception was thrown all the way back to where it was caught and handled:

```
java.io.FileNotFoundException: file.js (The system
cannot find the file specified)
 at java.io.FileInputStream.open(Native Method)
 at java.io.FileInputStream.(init)
 (FileInputSteam.java:106)
 at java.io.FileInputStream.(init)
 (FileInputSteam.java:66)
 at java.io.FileReader(init)(FileReader.java:41)
 at EHExample.openFile(EHExample.java:24)
 at EHExample.main(EHExample.java:15)
```

CHAPTER 8

Java Modifiers

Modifiers, which are Java keywords, may be applied to classes, interfaces, constructors, methods, and data members.

Table 8-1 lists the Java modifiers and their applicability. Note that private and protected classes are allowed, but only as inner or nested classes.

Table 8-1. Java modifiers

Modifier	Class	Interface	Constructor	Method	Data member
Access modifiers					
package-private	Yes	Yes	Yes	Yes	Yes
private	No	No	Yes	Yes	Yes
protected	No	No	Yes	Yes	Yes
public	Yes	Yes	Yes	Yes	Yes
Other modifiers					
abstract	Yes	Yes	No	Yes	No
final	Yes	No	No	Yes	Yes
native	No	No	No	Yes	No
strictfp	Yes	Yes	No	Yes	No
static	No	No	No	Yes	Yes
synchronized	No	No	No	Yes	No

Modifier	Class	Interface	Constructor	Method	Data member
transient	No	No	No	No	Yes
volatile	No	No	No	No	Yes

Inner classes may also use the private or protected access modifiers. Local variables may only use one modifier: final.

Access Modifiers

Access modifiers define the access privileges of classes, interfaces, constructors, methods, and data members. Access modifiers consist of public, private, and protected. If no modifier is present, the default access of *package-private* is used.

Table 8-2 provides details on visibility when access modifiers are used.

Table 8-2. Access modifiers and their visibility

Modifier	Visibility
package-private	The default *package-private* limits access from within the package.
private	The private method is accessible from within its class. The private data member is accessible from within its class. It can be indirectly accessed through methods (i.e., getter and setter methods).
protected	The protected method is accessible from within its package, and also from outside its package by subclasses of the class containing the method. The protected data member is accessible within its package, and also from outside its package by subclasses of the class containing the data member.
public	The public modifier allows access from anywhere, even outside of the package in which it was declared. Note that interfaces are public by default.

Other (Nonaccess) Modifiers

Table 8-3 contains the nonaccess Java modifiers and their usage.

Table 8-3. Nonaccess Java modifiers

Modifier	Usage
abstract	An abstract class is a class that is declared with the keyword abstract. It cannot be simultaneously declared with final. Interfaces are abstract by default and do not have to be declared abstract. An abstract method is a method that contains only a signature and no body. If at least one method in a class is abstract, then the enclosing class is abstract. It cannot be declared final, native, private, static, or synchronized.
final	A final class cannot be extended. A final method cannot be overridden. A final data member is initialized only once and cannot be changed. A data member that is declared static final is set at compile time and cannot be changed.
native	A native method is used to merge other programming languages such as C and C++ code into a Java program. It contains only a signature and no body. It cannot be used simultaneously with strictfp.
static	Both static methods and static variables are accessed through the class name. They are used for the whole class and all instantiations from that class. A static data member is accessed through the class name. Only one static data member exists no matter how many instances of the class exist.
strictfp	A strictfp class will follow the IEEE 754-1985 floating-point specification for all of its floating-point operations. A strictfp method has all expressions in the method as FP-strict. Methods within interfaces cannot be declared strictfp. It cannot be used simultaneously with the native modifier.

Modifier	Usage
synchronized	A synchronized method allows only one thread to execute the method block at a time, making it thread safe. Statements can also be synchronized.
transient	A transient data member is not serialized when the class is serialized. It is not part of the persistent state of an object.
volatile	A volatile data member informs a thread both to get the latest value for the variable, instead of using a cached copy, and to write all updates to the variable as they occur.

PART II
Platform

CHAPTER 9

Java Platform, SE

The Java Platform, Standard Edition, includes the Java Runtime Environment (JRE) and its encompassing Java Development Kit (JDK; see Chapter 10), the Java Programming Language, Java Virtual Machines (JVMs), tools/utilities, and the Java SE API libraries; see Figure 9-1.

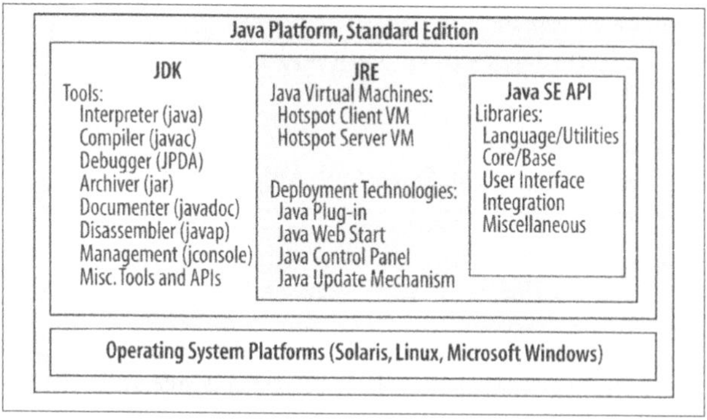

Figure 9-1. Java Platform, SE

Common Java SE API Libraries

Java SE API standard libraries are provided within packages. Each package is made up of classes and/or interfaces. An abbreviated list of commonly used packages is represented here.

Java SE provides the JavaFX Runtime libraries from Java SE 7 update 6 and JavaFX 2.2 onwards (*http://bit.ly/11NntXh*).

Language and Utility Libraries

`java.lang`
> Language support; system/math methods, fundamental types, strings, threads, and exceptions

`java.lang.annotation`
> Annotation framework; metadata library support

`java.lang.instrument`
> Program instrumentation; agent services to instrument JVM programs

`java.lang.invoke`
> Dynamic Language Support; supported by core classes and VM

`java.lang.management`
> Java Management Extensions API; JVM monitoring and management

`java.lang.ref`
> Reference-object classes; interaction support with the GC

`java.lang.reflect`
> Reflective information about classes and objects

`java.util`
> Utilities; collections, event model, date/time, and international support

`java.util.concurrent`
> Concurrency utilities; executors, queues, timing, and synchronizers

`java.util.concurrent.atomic`
> Atomic toolkit; lock-free thread-safe programming on single variables

`java.util.concurrent.locks`
> Locking framework; locks and conditions

`java.util.jar`
> Java Archive file format; reading and writing

`java.util.logging`
> Logging; failures, errors, performance issues, and bugs

`java.util.prefs`
> User and system preferences; retrieval and storage

`java.util.regex`
> Regular expressions; char sequences matched to patterns

`java.util.zip`
> ZIP and GZIP file formats; reading and writing

Base Libraries

`java.applet`
> Applet framework; embeddable window and control methods

`java.beans`
> Beans; components based on JavaBeans, long-term persistence

`java.beans.beancontext`
> Bean context; containers for beans, run environments

`java.io`
> Input/output; through data streams, the filesystem, and serialization

`java.math`

  Mathematics; extra large integer and decimal arithmetic

`java.net`

  Networking; TCP, UDP, sockets, and addresses

`java.nio`

  High performance I/O; buffers, memory-mapped files

`java.nio.channels`

  Channels for I/O; selectors for nonblocking I/O

`java.nio.charset`

  Character sets; translation between bytes and Unicode

`java.nio.file`

  File support; files, file attributes, filesystems

`java.nio.file.attribute`

  File and filesystem attribute support

`java.text`

  Text utilities; text, dates, numbers, and messages

`javax.annotation`

  Annotation types; library support

`javax.management`

  JMX API; application configuration, statistics, and state changes

`javax.net`

  Networking; socket factories

`javax.net.ssl`

  Secured sockets layer; error detection, data encryption/authentication

`javax.tools`

  Program invoked tool interfaces; compilers, file managers

Integration Libraries

`java.sql`
> Structured Query Language (SQL); access and processing data source information

`javax.jws`
> Java web services; supporting annotation types

`javax.jws.soap`
> Java web services; SOAP bindings and message parameters

`javax.naming`
> Naming services; Java Naming and Directory Interface (JNDI)

`javax.naming.directory`
> Directory services; JNDI operations for directory-stored objects

`javax.naming.event`
> Event services; JNDI event notification operations

`javax.naming.ldap`
> Lightweight Directory Access Protocol v3; operations and controls

`javax.script`
> Scripting language support; integration, bindings, and invocations

`javax.sql`
> SQL; database APIs and server-side capabilities

`javax.sql.rowset.serial`
> Serializable mappings; between SQL types and data types

`javax.sql.rowset`
> Java Database Connectivity (JDBC) Rowset; standard interfaces

```
javax.transactions.xa
```
XA Interface; transaction and resource manager contracts for JTA

User Interface Libraries: Miscellaneous

```
javax.accessibility
```
Accessibility technology; assistive support for UI components

```
javax.imageio
```
Java image I/O; image file content description (metadata, thumbnails)

```
javax.print
```
Print services; formatting and job submissions

```
javax.print.attribute
```
Java Print Services; attributes and attribute set collecting

```
javax.print.attribute.standard
```
Standard attributes; widely used attributes and values

```
javax.print.event
```
Printing events; services and print job monitoring

```
javax.sound.midi
```
Sound; I/O, sequencing, and synthesis of MIDI Types 0 and 1

```
javax.sound.sampled
```
Sound; sampled audio data (AIFF, AU, and WAV formats)

User Interface Libraries: Abstract Window Toolkit (AWT) API

```
java.awt
```
Abstract Window Toolkit; user interfaces, graphics, and images

`java.awt.color`
> AWT color spaces; International Color Consortium Profile Format Specs

`java.awt.datatransfer`
> AWT data transfers; between/within applications, clipboard support

`java.awt.dnd`
> AWT drag and drop; direct GUI manipulation gestures

`java.awt.event`
> AWT event listeners/adapters for events fired by AWT components

`java.awt.font`
> AWT fonts; Type 1 Multiple Master, Open Type and True Type fonts

`java.awt.geom`
> AWT geometry manipulation; two-dimensional support

`java.awt.im`
> AWT input method framework; text input, languages, and handwriting

`java.awt.image`
> AWT image streaming framework; image creation and modification

`java.awt.image.renderable`
> AWT rendering-independent images; production

`java.awt.print`
> AWT printing API; doc type specs, controls page setup/ formats

User Interface Libraries: Swing API

`javax.swing`
> Swing API; pure Java components (buttons, split panes, tables, etc.)

`javax.swing.border`
> Swing specialized borders; customized versus default Look-and-Feel borders

`javax.swing.colorchooser`
> Swing JColorChooser component support; color selection dialog box

`javax.swing.event`
> Swing events; event listeners and event adapters

`javax.swing.filechooser`
> Swing JFileChooser component support; filesystem dialog box

`javax.swing.plaf`
> Swing Pluggable Look-and-Feel; support for basic and Metal Look-and-Feels

`javax.swing.plaf.basic`
> Swing Basic Look-and-Feel; default Look-and-Feel behavior

`javax.swing.plaf.metal`
> Swing Metal Look-and-Feel; Metal/Steel Look-and-Feel

`javax.swing.plaf.multi`
> Swing Multiple Look-and-Feel; combines multiple Look-and-Feels

`javax.swing.plaf.nimbus`
> Swing Nimbus Look-and-Feel; cross-platform Look-and-Feel

`javax.swing.plaf.synth`
> Swing Skinnable Look-and-Feel; all painting is delegated

`javax.swing.table`
> Swing JTable component support; tabular data structures

`javax.swing.text`
> Swing text component support; editable and noneditable text components

---

`javax.swing.text.html`

Swing HTML text editors; HTML text editor creation support

`javax.swing.text.html.parser`

Swing HTML parsers; default HTML parser support

`javax.swing.text.rtf`

Swing Rich Text Format (RTF) text editors; editing support

`javax.swing.tree`

Swing JTree component support; construction, management, and rendering

`javax.swing.undo`

Swing undo/redo operations; text component support

Remote Method Invocation (RMI) and CORBA Libraries

`java.rmi`

Remote Method Invocation; invokes objects on remote JVMs

`java.rmi.activation`

RMI Object Activation; activates persistent remote object's references

`java.rmi.dgc`

RMI distributed garbage collection (DGC); remote object tracking from client

`java.rmi.registry`

RMI registry; remote object that maps names to remote objects

`java.rmi.server`

RMI server side; RMI Transport Protocol, Hypertext Transfer Protocol (HTTP) tunneling, stubs `javax.rmi`

> Remote Method Invocation; Remote Method Invocation; Internet InterORB Protocol (IIOP), RMI-IIOP, Java Remote Method Protocol (JRMP)

`javax.rmi.CORBA`

> Common Object Request Broker Architecture (CORBA) support; portability APIs for RMI-IIOP and Object Request Brokers (ORBs)

`javax.rmi.ssl`

> Secured Sockets Layer (SSL); RMI client and server support

`org.omg.CORBA`

> OMG CORBA; CORBA to Java mapping, ORBs

`org.omg.CORBA_2_3`

> OMG CORBA additions; further Java Compatibility Kit (JCK) test support

Security Libraries

`java.security`

> Security; algorithms, mechanisms, and protocols

`java.security.cert`

> Certifications; parsing, managing Certificate Revocation Lists (CRLs) and certification paths

`java.security.interfaces`

> Security interfaces: Rivest, Shamir, and Adelman (RSA) and Digital Signature Algorithm (DSA) generation

`java.security.spec`

> Specifications; security keys and algorithm parameters

`javax.crypto`

> Cryptographic operations; encryption, keys, MAC generations

`javax.crypto.interfaces`

> Diffie-Hellman keys; defined in RSA Laboratories' PKCS #3

`javax.crypto.spec`

Specifications; for security key and algorithm parameters

`javax.security.auth`

Security authentication and authorization; access controls specifications

`javax.security.auth.callback`

Authentication callback support; services interaction with apps

`javax.security.auth.kerberos`

Kerberos network authentication protocol; related utility classes

`javax.security.auth.login`

Login and configuration; pluggable authentication framework

`javax.security.auth.x500`

X500 Principal and X500 Private Credentials; subject storage

`javax.security.sasl`

Simple Authentication and Security Layer (SASL); SASL authentication

`org.ietf.jgss`

Java Generic Security Service (JGSS); authentication, data integrity

Extensible Markup Language (XML) Libraries

`javax.xml`

Extensible Markup Language (XML); constants

`javax.xml.bind`

XML runtime bindings; unmarshalling, marshalling, and validation `javax.xml.crypto`

XML cryptography; signature generation and data encryption

`javax.xml.crypto.dom`

XML and Document Object Model (DOM); cryptographic implementations

`javax.xml.crypto.dsig`

XML digital signatures; generating and validating

`javax.xml.datatype`

XML and Java data types; mappings

`javax.xml.namespace`

XML namespaces; processing

`javax.xml.parsers`

XML parsers; Simple API for XML (SAX) and DOM parsers

`javax.xml.soap`

XML; SOAP messages; creation and building

`javax.xml.transform`

XML transformation processing; no DOM or SAX dependency

`javax.xml.transform.dom`

XML transformation processing; DOM-specific API

`javax.xml.transform.sax`

XML transformation processing; SAX-specific API

`javax.xml.transform.stax`

XML transformation processing; Streaming API for XML (StAX) API

`javax.xml.validation`

XML validation; verification against XML schema

`javax.xml.ws`

Java API for XML Web Services (JAX-WS); core APIs

`javax.xml.ws.handler`

> JAX-WS message handlers; message context and handler interfaces

`javax.xml.ws.handler.soap`

> JAX-WS; SOAP message handlers

`javax.xml.ws.http`

> JAX-WS; HTTP bindings

`javax.xml.ws.soap`

> JAX-WS; SOAP bindings

`javax.xml.xpath`

> XPath expressions; evaluation and access

`org.w3c.dom`

> W3C's DOM; file content and structure access and updates

`org.xml.sax`

> XML.org's SAX; file content and structure access and updates

CHAPTER 10

Development Basics

The Java Runtime Environment (JRE) provides the backbone for running Java applications. The Java Development Kit (JDK) provides all of the components and necessary resources to develop Java applications.

Java Runtime Environment

The JRE is a collection of software that allows a computer system to run a Java application. The software collection consists of the Java Virtual Machines (JVMs) that interpret Java bytecode into machine code, standard class libraries, user interface toolkits, and a variety of utilities.

Java Development Kit

The JDK is a programming environment for compiling, debugging, and running Java applications, Java Beans, and Java applets. The JDK includes the JRE with the addition of the Java Programming Language and additional development tools and tool APIs. Oracle's JDK supports Mac OS X, Solaris, Linux (Oracle, Suse, Red Hat, Ubuntu, and Debian (on ARM)), and Microsoft Windows (Server 2008, Server 2012, XP, Vista, 7, and 8). Additional operating system and special purpose JVMs, JDKs, and JREs are freely available at *http://java-virtual-machine.net/other.html*.

Browsers supported are Internet Explorer (7.x, 8.x, 9.x, and 10.x), Mozilla Firefox (3.6 and above), Chrome, and Safari (5.1.3 and above).

Table 10-1 lists versions of the JDK provided by Oracle. Download the most recent version at Oracle's website (*http://bit.ly/16mhImY*), where you can also download older versions (*http://bit.ly/16mhHzq*).

Table 10-1. Java Development Kits

Java Development Kits	Codename	Release	Packages	Classes
Java SE 7 with JDK 1.7.0	Dolphin	2011	209	4,024
Java SE 6 with JDK 1.6.0	Mustang	2006	203	3,793
Java 2 SE 5.0 with JDK 1.5.0	Tiger	2004	166	3,279
Java 2 SE with SDK 1.4.0	Merlin	2002	135	2,991
Java 2 SE with SDK 1.3	Kestrel	2000	76	1,842
Java 2 with SDK 1.2	Playground	1998	59	1,520
Development Kit 1.1	---	1997	23	504
Development Kit 1.0	Oak	1996	8	212

Java SE version 6 reached Oracle's End of Public Updates in November 2012.

Java Program Structure

Java source files are created with text editors such as jEdit, TextPad, Vim, Notepad++, or one provided by a Java Integrated Development Environment (IDE). The source files must have the *.java* extension and the same name as the public class name contained in the file. If the class has *package-private* access, the class name can differ from the filename.

Therefore, a source file named *HelloWorld.java* would correspond to the public class named HelloWorld, as represented in the following example (all nomenclature in Java is case-sensitive):

```
1 package com.oreilly.tutorial;
2 import java.util.*;
3 // import java.util.Calendar;
4 // import java.util.GregorianCalendar;
5
6 public class HelloWorld
7 {
8   public static void main(String[] args)
9   {
10      Calendar calendar =
          GregorianCalendar.getInstance();
11      System.out.print(calendar.getTime());
12      System.out.println(" - Hello, World!");
13  }
14 }
```

In line 1, the class HelloWorld is contained in the package *com.oreilly.tutorial*. This package name implies that *com/oreilly/tutorial* is a directory structure that is accessible on the class path for the compiler and the runtime environment. Packaging source files is optional, but it is recommended to avoid conflicts with other software packages.

In line 2, the import declaration allows for the JVM to search for classes from other packages. Here, the asterisk allows for all classes in the java.util package to be made available. However, you should always explicitly include classes so that dependencies are documented; including the statements import java.util.Calendar; and import java.util.GregorianCalendar;, which as you see are currently commented out, would have been a better choice than simply using import java.util.*;. Note that import statements are not needed at all, as one may include the full package name before each class name, but this is not an ideal way to code.

TIP

The java.lang package is the only Java package imported by default.

In line 6, there must be only one top-level `public` class defined in a source file. In addition, the file may include multiple top-level *package-private* classes.

Looking at line 8, we note that Java applications must have a `main` method. This method is the entry point into a Java program, and it must be defined. The modifiers must be declared `public`, `static`, and `void`. The arguments parameter provides a string array of command-line arguments.

TIP

Container-managed application components (e.g., Spring and Java EE) do not have a `main` method.

In lines 11 and 12, the statements provide calls to the `System.out.print` and `System.out.println` methods to print out the supplied text to the console window.

Command-Line Tools

A JDK provides several command-line tools that aid in software development. Commonly used tools include the compiler, launcher/interpreter, archiver, and documenter. Find a complete list of tools at Oracle.com (*http://bit.ly/16mhHQ3*).

Java Compiler

The Java compiler translates Java source files into Java bytecode. The compiler creates a bytecode file with the same name as the source file but with the *.class* extension. Here is a list of commonly used compiler options:

```
javac [-options] [source files]
```
This is the usage to compile Java source files.

```
javac HelloWorld.java
```
This basic usage compiles the program to produce *Hello-World.class*.

```
javac -cp /dir/Classes/ HelloWorld.java
```
The -cp and -classpath options are equivalent and identify classpath directories to utilize at compile time.

```
javac -d /opt/hwapp/classes HelloWorld.java
```
The -d option places generated class files into a preexisting specified directory. If there is a package definition, the path will be included (i.e., */opt/hwapp/src/com/oreilly/tutorial/*).

```
javac -s /opt/hwapp/src HelloWorld.java
```
The -s option places generated source files into a preexisting specified directory. If there is a package definition, the path will be further expanded (i.e., */opt/hwapp/src/com/oreilly/tutorial/*).

```
javac -source 1.4 HelloWorld.java
```
The -source option provides source compatibility with the given release, allowing unsupported keywords to be used as identifiers.

```
javac -X
```
The -X option prints a synopsis of nonstandard options. For example, -Xlint:unchecked enables recommended warnings, printing out further details for unchecked or unsafe operations.

TIP

Even though -Xlint and other -X options are commonly found among Java compilers, the -X options are not standardized, so their availability across JDKs should not be assumed.

```
javac -version
```
The -version option prints the version of the javac utility.

```
javac -help
```
The -help option, or the absence of arguments, will cause the help information for the javac command to be printed.

Java Interpreter

The Java interpreter handles the program execution, including launching the application. Here is a list of commonly used interpreter options.

```
java [-options] class [arguments...]
```
This is the usage to run the interpreter.

```
java [-options] -jar jarfile [arguments...]
```
This is the usage to execute a JAR file.

```
java HelloWorld
```
This basic usage starts the JRE, loads the class HelloWorld, and runs the main method of the class.

```
java com.oreilly.tutorial.HelloWorld
```
This basic usage starts the JRE, loads the HelloWorld class under the *com/oreilly/tutorial/* directory, and runs the main method of the class.

```
java -cp /tmp/Classes HelloWorld
```
The -cp and -classpath options identify classpath directories to utilize at runtime.

```
java -Dsun.java2d.ddscale=true HelloWorld
```
The -D option sets a system property value. Here, hardware accelerator scaling is turned on.

```
java -ea HelloWorld
```
The -ea and -enableassertions options enable Java assertions. Assertions are diagnostic code that you insert in your application. For more information on assertions, see "Assert Statement" on page 62 in Chapter 6.

```
java -da HelloWorld
```
> The -da and -disableassertions options disable Java assertions.

```
java -client HelloWorld
```
> The -client option selects the client virtual machine (versus the server virtual machine) to enhance interactive applications such as GUIs.

```
java -server HelloWorld
```
> The -server option selects the server virtual machine (versus the client virtual machine) to enhance overall system performance.

```
java -splash:images/world.gif HelloWorld
```
> The -splash option accepts an argument to display a splash screen of an image prior to running the application.

```
java -version
```
> The -version option prints the version of the Java interpreter, the JRE, and the virtual machine.

```
java [-d32 | -d64]
```
> The [-d32] and the [-d64] options call for the use of the 32-bit or the 64-bit data model (respectively), if available.

```
java -help
```
> The -help option, or the absence of arguments, will cause the help information for the java command to be printed.

```
javaw <classname>
```
> On the Windows OS, javaw is equivalent to the java command but without a console window. The Linux equivalent is accomplished by running the java command as a background process with the ampersand, java <classname> &.

Java Program Packager

The Java Archive (JAR) utility is an archiving and compression tool, typically used to combine multiple files into a single file called a JAR file. JAR consists of a ZIP archive containing a manifest file (JAR content describer) and optional signature files (for security). Here is a list of commonly used JAR options along with examples:

```
jar [options] [jar-file] [manifest-files] [entry-point]
[-C dir] files...
```
This is the usage for the JAR utility.

```
jar cf files.jar HelloWorld.java com/oreilly/tutorial/
HelloWorld.class
```
The c option allows for the creation of a JAR file. The f option allows for the specification of the filename. In this example, *HelloWorld.java* and *com/oreilly/tutorial/Hello-World.class* are included in the JAR file.

```
jar tfv files.jar
```
The t option is used to list the table of contents of the JAR file. The f option is used to specify the filename. The v option lists the contents in verbose format.

```
jar xf files.jar
```
The x option allows for the extraction of the contents of the JAR file. The f option allows for the specification of the filename.

TIP

Several other ZIP tools (e.g., 7-Zip, WinZip, and Win-RAR) can work with JAR files.

JAR File Execution

JAR files can be created so that they are executable by specifying the file within the JAR where the "main" class resides, so the Java interpreter knows which `main()` method to utilize. Here is a complete example of making a JAR file executable:

1. Create a *HelloWorld.java* file from the `HelloWorld` class at the beginning of this chapter.

2. Create the subfolders *com/oreilly/tutorial/*.

3. Run `javac HelloWorld`.

    Use this command to compile the program and place the *HelloWorld.class* file into the *com/oreilly/tutorial/* directory.

4. Create a file *Manifest.txt* in the directory where the package is located. In the file, include the following line specifying where the main class is located:

    ```
    Main-Class: com.oreilly.tutorial.HelloWorld
    ```

5.

    Run `jar cmf Manifest.txt helloWorld.jar com/oreilly/tutorial`.

    Use this command to create a JAR file that adds the *Manifest.txt* contents to the manifest file, *MANIFEST.MF*. The manifest file is also used to define extensions and various package-related data:

    ```
    Manifest-Version: 1.0
    Created-By: 1.7.0 (Oracle Corporation)
    Main-Class: com.oreilly.tutorial.HelloWorld
    ```

6. Run `jar tf HelloWorld.jar`.

    Use this command to display the contents of the JAR file:

    ```
    META-INF/
    META-INF/MANIFEST.MF
    com/
    com/oreilly/
    com/oreilly/tutorial
    com/oreilly/tutorial/HelloWorld.class
    ```

7. Finally, run `java -jar HelloWorld.jar`.

    Use this command to execute the JAR file.

Java Documenter

Javadoc is a command-line tool used to generate documentation on source files. The documentation is more detailed when the appropriate Javadoc comments are applied to the source code; see "Comments" on page 9 in Chapter 2. Here is a list of commonly used javadoc options and examples:

`javadoc [options] [packagenames] [sourcefiles]`
> This is the usage to produce Java documentation.

`javadoc HelloWorld.java`
> The javadoc command generates HTML documentation files: *HelloWorld.html*, *index.html*, *allclaases-frame.html*, *constant-values.html*, *deprecated-list.html*, *overview-tree.html*, *package-summary.html*, etc.

`javadoc -verbose HelloWorld.java`
> The -verbose option provides more details while Javadoc is running.

`javadoc -d /tmp/ HelloWorld.java`
> This -d option specifies the directory where the generated HTML files will be extracted to. Without this option, the files will be placed in the current working directory.

`javadoc -sourcespath /Classes/ Test.java`
> The -sourcepath option specifies where to find user *.java* source files.

`javadoc -exclude <pkglist> Test.java`
> The -exclude option specifies which packages not to generate HTML documentation files for.

`javadoc -public Test.java`
> The -public option produces documentation for public classes and members.

`javadoc -protected Test.java`
> The -protected option produces documentation for protected and public classes and members. This is the default setting.

```
javadoc -package Test.java
```
> The -package option produces documentation for package, protected, and public classes and members.

```
javadoc -private Test.java
```
> The -private option produces documentation for all classes and members.

```
javadoc -help
```
> The -help option, or the absence of arguments, causes the help information for the javadoc command to be printed.

Classpath

The classpath is an argument set, used by several command-line tools, that tells the JVM where to look for user-defined classes and packages. Classpath conventions differ among operating systems.

On Microsoft Windows operating systems, directories within paths are delineated with backslashes, and the semicolon is used to separate the paths:

```
-classpath \home\XClasses\;dir\YClasses\;.
```

On POSIX-compliant operations systems (e.g., Solaris, Linux, and Mac OS X), directories within paths are delineated with forward slashes and the colon is used to separate the paths:

```
-classpath /home/XClasses/:dir/YClasses/:.
```

TIP

The period represents the current working directory.

The CLASSPATH environmental variable can also be set to tell the Java compiler where to look for class files and packages:

```
rem Windows
set CLASSPATH=classpath1;classpath2

# Linux, Solaris, Mac OS X
    # (May vary due to shell specifics)
    setenv CLASSPATH classpath1:classpath2
```

CHAPTER 11

Memory Management

Java has automatic memory management, which is also known as garbage collection (GC). GC's principal tasks are allocating memory, maintaining referenced objects in memory, and recovering memory from objects that no longer have references to them.

Garbage Collectors

Since the J2SE 5.0 release, the Java HotSpot Virtual Machine performs self-tuning. This process includes the attempted best-fit GC and related settings at startup, based on platform information, as well as ongoing GC tuning.

Although the initial settings and runtime tuning for GC are generally successful, there are times when you may wish to change or tune your GC based on the following goals:

Maximum pause time goal
> The maximum pause time goal is the desired time that the GC pauses the application to recover memory.

Throughput goal
> The throughput goal is the desired application time, or the time spent outside of GC.

The following sections provide an overview of various garbage collectors, their main focus, and situations in which they should be used. "Command-Line Options" on page 114 explains how to acquire information for manually selecting the GC.

Serial Collector

The serial collector is performed via a single thread on a single CPU. When this GC thread is run, the execution of the application will pause until the collection is complete.

This collection is best used when your application has a small data set up to approximately 100 MB and does not have a requirement for low pause times.

Parallel Collector

The parallel collector, also known as the throughput collector, can be performed with multiple threads across several CPUs. Using these multiple threads significantly speeds up GC.

This collector is best used when there are no pause time constraints and application performance is the most important aspect of your program.

Parallel Compacting Collector

The parallel compacting collector is similar to the parallel collector except for refined algorithms that reduce collection pause times.

This collector is best used for applications that do have pause time constraints.

TIP

The parallel compacting collector is available beginning with J2SE 5.0 update 6.

Concurrent Mark-Sweep (CMS) Collector

The CMS, also known as the low-latency collector, implements algorithms to handle large collections that may warrant long pauses.

This collector is best used when response times take precedence over throughput times and GC pauses.

Garbage-First (G1) Collector

The Garbage-First collector, also known as the G1 collector, is used for multiprocessor machines with large memories. This server-style GC meets pause time goals with high probability, while achieving high throughput. Whole-heap operations (e.g., global marking) are performed concurrently with the application threads preventing interruptions proportional to the heap or live-data size.

TIP

The Garbage-First collector is available beginning with Java SE 7 update 4. Its goal is to replace the CMS collector.

Memory Management Tools

Although tuning your GC may prove to be successful, it is important to note that the GCs do not provide guarantees, only goals; any improvement gained on one platform may be undone on another. It is best to find the source of the problem with memory management tools, including profilers.

Table 11-1 lists such tools. All are command-line applications except HPROF (Heap/CPU Profiling Tool). HPROF is dynamically loaded from a command-line option. The following example returns a complete list of options that can be passed to HPROF:

```
java -agentlib:hprof=help
```

Table 11-1. JDK memory management tools

Resource	Description
jvisualvm	All-in-one Java troubleshooting tool (*http://visualvm.java.net/*)
jconsole	Java Management Extensions (JMX)-compliant monitoring tool
jinfo	Configuration information tool
jmap	Memory map tool
jstack	Stack trace tool
jstat	JVM statistics monitoring tool
jhat	Heap analysis tool
HPROF Profiler	CPU usage, heap statistics, and monitor contentions profiler
jdb	Java debugger tool

TIP

To determine which GC is being used, you can view the information in the JConsole application.

Command-Line Options

The following GC-related command-line options can be passed into the Java interpreter to interface with the functionality of the Java HotSpot Virtual Machine (for a more complete list of options, visit Java HotSpot VM Options (*http://bit.ly/16mhL27*)):

`-XX:+PrintGC` *or* `-verbose:gc`
Prints out general information about the heap and garbage collection at each collection.

`-XX:+PrintCommandLineFlags -version`
Prints out heap settings, applied -XX values, and version information.

`-XX:+PrintGCDetails`

Prints out detailed information about the heap and garbage collection during each collection.

`-XX:+PrintGCTimeStamps`

Adds timestamps to the output from PrintGC or PrintGCDetails.

`-XX:+UseSerialGC`

Enables the serial collector.

`-XX:+UseParallelGC`

Enables the parallel collector.

`-XX:+UseParallelOldGC`

Enables the parallel compacting collector. Note that Old refers to the fact that new algorithms are used for "old" generation GC.

`-XX:+UseParNewGC`

Enables the parallel young generation collector. Can be used with the concurrent low pause collector.

`-XX:+UseConcMarkSweepGC`

Enables the concurrent low pause CMS collector. Can be used with the parallel young generation collector.

`-XX:+UseG1GC`

Enables the Garbage-First collector.

`-XX:+DisableExplicitGC`

Disables the explicit GC (System.gc()) methods.

`-XX:ParallelGCThreads=[`*threads*`]`

Defines the number of GC threads. The default correlates to the number of CPUs. This option applies to the CMS and parallel collectors.

`-XX:MaxGCPauseMillis=[`*milliseconds*`]`

Provides a hint to the GC for the desired maximum pause time goal in milliseconds. This option applies to the parallel collectors.

`-XX:+GCTimeRatio=[value]`

Provides a hint to the GC for the desired ratio of GC time to application time (1 / (1 + [value])) for the desired throughput goal. The default value is 99. This means that the application will run 99% of the time and therefore, the GC will run one percent of the time. This option applies to the parallel collectors.

`-XX:+CMSIncrementalMode`

Enables incremental mode for the CMS collector only. Used for machines with one or two processors.

`-XX:+CMSIncrementalPacing`

Enables automatic packing for the CMS collector only.

`-XX:MinHeapFreeRatio=[percent]`

Sets the minimum target percent for the proportion of free space to total heap size. The default percent is 40.

`-XX:MaxHeapFreeRatio=[percent]`

Sets the maximum target percent for the proportion of free space to total heap size. The default percent is 70.

`-Xms[bytes]`

Overrides the minimum heap size in bytes. Default: 1/64th of the system's physical memory up to 1 GB. Initial heap size is 4 MB for machines that are not server-class.

`-Xmx[bytes]`

Overrides the maximum heap size in bytes. Default: Smaller than 1/4th physical memory or 1 GB. Maximum heap size is 64 MB for machines that are not server-class.

`-Xmn[bytes]`

The size of the heap for the young generation.

`-XX:OnError=[command_line_tool [options]]`

Used to specify user-supplied scripts or commands when a fatal error occurs.

```
-XX+AggressiveOpts
```
Enables performance optimizations that are expected to be on by default in future releases.

TIP

Byte values include [k|K] for kilobytes, [m|M] for megabytes, and [g|G] for gigabytes.

Note that -XX options are not guaranteed to be stable. They are not part of the Java Language Specification (JLS) and are unlikely to be available in exact form and function from other third-party JVMs, if at all.

Resizing the JVM Heap

The heap is an area in memory that stores all objects created by an executing Java program. You should resize the heap only if it needs to be sized larger than the default heap size. If you are having performance problems or seeing the error message `java.lang.OutOfMemoryError`, you may be running out of heap space.

Interfacing with the GC

Interfacing with the garbage collector can be done through explicit invocation or via overriding the `finalize` method.

Explicit Garbage Collection

The garbage collector can be explicitly requested to be invoked with `System.gc()` or `Runtime.getRuntime().gc()`. However, explicit invocation of the GC should generally be avoided because it could force full collections (when a minor collection may suffice), thereby unnecessarily increasing the pause times. The request for System.gc() is not always fulfilled as the JVM can and does ignore it at times.

Finalization

Every object has a finalize() method inherited from class Object. The garbage collector, prior to destroying the object, can invoke this method, but this invocation is not guaranteed. The default implementation of the finalize() method does nothing and although it is not recommended, the method can be overridden:

```java
public class TempClass extends SuperClass {
  ...
  // Performed when Garbage Collection occurs
  protected void finalize() throws Throwable {
    try {
      /* Desired functionality goes here */
    } finally {
      // Optionally, you can call the
      // finalize method of the superclass
      super.finalize(); // From SuperClass
    }
  }
}
```

The following example destroys an object:

```java
public class MainClass {
  public static void main(String[] args) {
    TempClass t = new TempClass();
    // Object has references removed
    t = null;
    // GC made available
    System.gc();
  }
}
```

CHAPTER 12

Basic Input and Output

Java provides several classes for basic input and output, a few of which are discussed in this chapter. The basic classes can be used to read and write to files, sockets, and the console. They also provide for working with files and directories and for serializing data. Java I/O classes throw exceptions, including the IOException, which needs to be handled.

Java I/O classes also support formatting data, compressing and decompressing streams, encrypting and decrypting, and communicating between threads using piped streams.

The new I/O (NIO) APIs that were introduced in Java 1.4 provide additional I/O capabilities, including buffering, file locking, regular expression matching, scalable networking, and buffer management.

NIO 2.0 was introduced with Java SE 7 and is covered in the next chapter. NIO 2.0 extends NIO and provides a new filesystem API.

Standard Streams in, out, and err

Java uses three standard streams: in, out, and err.

System.in is the standard input stream that is used to get data from the user to a program:

```
byte teamName[] = new byte[200];
int size = System.in.read(teamName);
System.out.write(teamName,0,size);
```

System.out is the standard output stream that is used to output data from a program to the user:

```
System.out.print("Team complete");
```

System.err is the standard error stream that is used to output error data from a program to the user:

```
System.err.println("Not enough players");
```

Note that each of these methods can throw an IOException.

TIP

The Console class, introduced in Java SE 6, provides an alternative to the standard streams for interacting with the command-line environment.

Class Hierarchy for Basic Input and Output

Figure 12-1 shows a class hierarchy for commonly used readers, writers, and input and output streams. Note that I/O classes can be chained together to get multiple effects.

The Reader and Writer classes are used for reading and writing character data (text). The InputStream and OutputStream classes are typically used for reading and writing binary data.

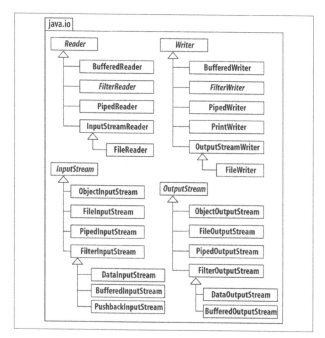

Figure 12-1. Common readers, writers, and input/output streams

File Reading and Writing

Java provides facilities to easily read and write to system files.

Reading Character Data from a File

To read character data from a file, use a BufferedReader. A FileReader can also be used, but it will not be as efficient if there is a large amount of data. The call to readLine() reads a line of text from the file. When reading is complete, call close() on the BufferedReader:

```
BufferedReader bReader = new BufferedReader
    (new FileReader("Master.txt"));
String lineContents;
```

```
while ((lineContents = bReader.readLine())
       != null) {...}
bReader.close();
```

Reading Binary Data from a File

To read binary data, use a `DataInputStream`. The call to `read()` reads the data from the input stream. Note that if only an array of bytes will be read, you should just use `InputStream`:

```
DataInputStream inStream = new DataInputStream
    (new FileInputStream("Team.bin"));
inStream.read();
```

If a large amount of data is going to be read, you should also use a `BufferedInputStream` to make reading the data more efficient:

```
DataInputStream inStream = new DataInputStream
(new BufferedInputStream(new FileInputStream(team)));
```

Binary data that has been read can be put back on the stream using methods in the `PushbackInputStream` class:

```
unread(int i);     // pushback a single byte
unread(byte[] b); // pushback array of bytes
```

Writing Character Data to a File

To write character data to a file, use a `PrintWriter`. Call the `close()` method of class `PrintWriter` when writing to the output stream is complete:

```
String in = "A huge line of text";
PrintWriter pWriter = new PrintWriter
  (new FileWriter("CoachList.txt"));
pWriter.println(in);
pWriter.close();
```

Text can also be written to a file using a `FileWriter` if there is a small amount of text to be written. Note that if the file passed into the `FileWriter` does not exist, it will automatically be created:

```
FileWriter fWriter = new
  FileWriter("CoachList.txt");
```

```
fwriter.write("This is the coach list.");
fwriter.close();
```

Writing Binary Data to a File

To write binary data, use a DataOutputStream. The call to write Int() writes an array of integers to the output stream:

```
File positions = new File("Positions.bin");
Int[] pos = {0, 1, 2, 3, 4};
DataOutputStream outStream = new DataOutputStream
    (new FileOutputStream(positions));
for (int i = 0; i < pos.length; i++)
  outStream.writeInt(pos[i]);
```

If a large amount of data is going to be written, then also use a BufferedOutputStream:

```
DataOutputStream outStream = new DataOutputStream
(new BufferedOutputStream(positions));
```

Socket Reading and Writing

Java provides facilities to easily read and write to system sockets.

Reading Character Data from a Socket

To read character data from a socket, connect to the socket and then use a BufferedReader to read the data:

```
Socket socket = new Socket("127.0.0.1", 64783);
InputStreamReader reader = new InputStreamReader
    (socket.getInputStream());
BufferedReader bReader = new BufferedReader(reader);
String msg = bReader.readLine();
```

Reading Binary Data from a Socket

To read binary data, use a DataInputStream. The call to read() reads the data from the input stream. Note that Socket class is located in java.net:

```
Socket socket = new Socket("127.0.0.1", 64783);
DataInputStream inStream = new DataInputStream
    (socket.getInputStream());
inStream.read();
```

If a large amount of data is going to be read, then also use a
BufferedInputStream to make reading the data more efficient:

```
DataInputStream inStream = new DataInputStream
(new BufferedInputStream(socket.getInputStream()));
```

Writing Character Data to a Socket

To write character data to a socket, make a connection to a socket
and then create and use a PrintWriter to write the character data
to the socket:

```
Socket socket = new Socket("127.0.0.1", 64783);
PrintWriter pWriter = new PrintWriter
    (socket.getOutputStream());
pWriter.println("Dad, we won the game.");
```

Writing Binary Data to a Socket

To write binary data, use a DataOutputStream. The call to write()
writes the data to an output stream:

```
byte positions[] = new byte[10];
Socket socket = new Socket("127.0.0.1", 64783);
DataOutputStream outStream = new DataOutputStream
    (socket.getOutputStream());
outStream.write(positions, 0, 10);
```

If a large amount of data is going to be written, then also use a
BufferedOutputStream:

```
DataOutputStream outStream = new DataOutputStream
(new BufferedOutputStream(socket.getOutputStream()));
```

Serialization

To save a version of an object (and all related data that would need
to be restored) as an array of bytes, the class of this object must

implement the interface Serializable. Note that data members declared transient will not be included in the serialized object. Use caution when using serialization and deserialization, as changes to a class—including moving the class in the class hierarchy, deleting a field, changing a field to nontransient or static, and using different JVMs—can all impact restoring an object.

The ObjectOutputStream and ObjectInputStream classes can be used to serialize and deserialize objects.

Serialize

To serialize an object, use an ObjectOutputStream:

```
ObjectOutputStream s = new
  ObjectOutputStream(new FileOutputStream("p.ser"));
```

An example of serializing follows:

```
ObjectOutputStream oStream = new
  ObjectOutputStream(new
  FileOutputStream("PlayerDat.ser"));
oStream.writeObject(player);
oStream.close();
```

Deserialize

To deserialize an object (i.e., turn it from a flattened version of an object to an object), use an ObjectInputStream, then read in the file and cast the data into the appropriate object.

```
ObjectInputStream d = new
  ObjectInputStream(new FileInputStream("p.ser"));
```

An example of deserializing follows:

```
ObjectInputStream iStream = new
    ObjectInputStream(new
    FileInputStream("PlayerDat.ser"));
Player p = (Player) iStream.readObject();
```

Zipping and Unzipping Files

Java provides classes for creating compressed ZIP and GZIP files. ZIP archives multiple files, whereas GZIP archives a single file.

Use `ZipOutputStream` to zip files and `ZipInputSteam` to unzip them:

```java
ZipOutputStream zipOut = new ZipOutputStream(
    new FileOutputStream("out.zip"));
String[] fNames = new String[] {"f1", "f2"};
for (int i = 0; i < fNames.length; i++) {
ZipEntry entry = new ZipEntry(fNames[i]);
File InputStream fin =
    new FileInputStream(fNames[i]);
try {
  zipOut.putNextEntry(entry);
  for (int a = fin.read();
    a != -1; a = fin.read()) {
        zipOut.write(a);
  }
  fin.close();
  zipOut.close();
 } catch (IOException ioe) {...}
}
```

To unzip a file, create a `ZipInputStream`, call its `getNextEntry()` method, and read the file into an `OutputStream`.

Compressing and Uncompressing GZIP Files

To compress a GZIP file, create a new `GZIPOutputStream`, pass it the name of a file with the *.gzip* extension, and then transfer the data from the `GZIPOutputStream` to the `FileInputStream`.

To uncompress a GZIP file, create a `GZipInputStream`, create a new `FileOutputStream`, and read the data into it.

File and Directory Handling

Java provides the File class for working with files and directories, including accessing existing files, searching files, creating directories, listing the contents of a directory, and deleting files and directories.

Commonly Used Methods in the File Class

Table 12-1 contains a summary of the commonly used methods used in the File class.

Table 12-1. Commonly used methods in the File class

Method	Description
delete()	Deletes a file or directory
exists()	Checks if a file exists
list()	Lists contents of a directory
mkdir()	Makes a directory
renameTo(File f)	Renames a file

Accessing Existing Files

Existing files can be accessed using the File class. The File class represents a file or a directory; however, it does not have access to file contents.

To create a File object using just a filename, use the following code:

```
File roster = new File("Roster.txt");
```

To create a File object using a directory and a filename, use the following code:

```
File rosterDir = new File("/usr/rosters");
File roster = new File(rosterDir, "Roster.txt");
```

Seeking in Files

To read and write data at a given position in a file, use the method seek() in class RandomAccessFile. A RandomAccessFile is often created as "read" or "read/write," denoted by r and rw in the call to the RandomAccessFile constructor. Most random access files are fixed-record length binary files:

```
File team = new File("Team.txt");
RandomAccessFile raf = new
    RandomAccessFile(team, "rw");
raf.seek(10);
byte data = raf.readByte();
```

CHAPTER 13

NIO 2.0 Quicklook

NIO 2.0 was introduced with JDK 7 to provide enhanced file I/O support and access to the default filesystem. NIO 2.0 is supported by the `java.nio.file` and `java.nio.file.attribute` packages. The NIO 2.0 API is also known as "JSR 203: More New I/O APIs for the Java Platform." Popular interfaces that are used from the API are `Path`, `PathMatcher`, `FileVisitor`, and `WatchService`. Popular classes that are used from the API are `Paths` and `Files`.

The Path Interface

The `Path` interface can be used to operate on file and directory paths. This class is an upgraded version of the `java.io.File` class. The following code demonstrates the use of some of the methods of the `Path` interface and the `Paths` class for acquiring information:

```
Path p = Paths.get("/opt/jpgTools/README.txt");
System.out.println(p.getParent()); // \opt\jpgTools
System.out.println(p.getRoot()); // \
System.out.println(p.getNameCount()); // 3
System.out.println(p.getName(0)); // opt
System.out.println(p.getName(1)); // jpgTools
System.out.println(p.getFileName()); // README.txt
System.out.println(p.toString()); // The full path
```

The Path class also provides additional features, some of which are detailed in Table 13-1.

Table 13-1. Path interface capabilities

Path method	Capability
path.toUri()	Converts a path to a URI object
path.resolve(Path)	Combines two paths together
path.relativize(Path)	Constructs a path from one location to another
path.compareTo(Path)	Compares two paths against each other

The Files Class

The Files class can be used to check, delete, copy, or move a file or directory. The following code demonstrates some commonly used methods of the Files class:

```
// Intstantiate path objects
Path target1 = Paths.get("/opt/jpg/README1.txt");
Path p1 = Files.createFile(target1);
Path target2 = Paths.get("/opt/jpg/README2.txt");
Path p2 = Files.createFile(target2);
// Check file attributes
System.out.println(Files.isReadable(p1));
System.out.println(Files.isReadable(p2));
System.out.println(Files.isExecutable(p1));
System.out.println(Files.isSymbolicLink(p1));
System.out.println(Files.isWritable(p1));
System.out.println(Files.isHidden(p1));
System.out.println(Files.isSameFile(p1, p2));
// Delete, move and copy examples
Files.delete(p2);
System.out.println(Files.move(p1, p2));
System.out.println(Files.copy(p2, p1));
Files.delete(p1);
Files.delete(p2);
```

The `move` method accepts the varargs enumeration using `REPLACE_EXISTING` or `ATOMIC_MOVE`. `REPLACE_EXISTING` moves the file, even if it already exists. `ATOMIC_MOVE` ensures that any process watching the directory will be able to access the complete file.

The `copy` method accepts the varargs enumeration with `REPLACE_EXISTING`, `COPY_ATTRIBUTES`, or `NOFOLLOW_LINKS`. `REPLACE_EXISTING` copies the file, even if it already exists. `COPY_ATTRIBUTES` copies the file attributes. `NOFOLLOW_LINKS` copies the links, but not the targets.

Additional Features

The NIO 2.0 API also provides the following features, which are good to know for the job. Questions about these features are also included on the Oracle Certified Professional Java SE 7 Programmer Exam. These items are not covered here as they are more suited to a tutorial style guide or resource:

- The ability to find files using the `PathMatcher` interface.
- The ability to watch a directory using the `WatchService` interface.
- The ability to recursively access directory trees using the `FileVisitor` interface.

TIP

Consider reviewing *Pro Java 7 NIO.2* by Anghel Leonard (Apress, 2011) for comprehensive information on NIO 2.0.

CHAPTER 14

Concurrency

Threads in Java allow the use of multiple processors or multiple cores in one processor more efficiently. On a single processor, threads provide for concurrent operations such as overlapping I/O with processing.

Java supports multithreaded programming features with the `Thread` class and the `Runnable` interface.

Creating Threads

Threads can be created two ways, either by extending `java.lang.Thread` or by implementing `java.lang.Runnable`.

Extending the Thread Class

Extending the `Thread` class and overriding the `run()` method can create a threadable class. This is an easy way to start a thread:

```java
class Comet extends Thread {
  public void run() {
    System.out.println("Orbiting");
    orbit();
  }
}

Comet halley = new Comet();
```

Remember that only one superclass can be extended, so a class that extends Thread cannot extend any other superclass.

Implementing the Runnable Interface

Implementing the Runnable interface and defining its run() method can also create a threadable class. Creating a new Thread object and passing it an instance of the runnable class creates the thread:

```
class Asteroid implements Runnable {
  public void run() {
    System.out.println("Orbiting");
    orbit();
  }
}

Asteroid maja = new Asteroid();
Thread majaThread = new Thread(maja);
```

A single runnable instance can be passed to multiple thread objects. Each thread performs the same task:

```
Asteroid pallas = new Asteroid();
Thread pallasThread1 = new Thread(pallas);
Thread pallasThread2 = new Thread(pallas);
```

Thread States

Enumeration Thread.state provides six thread states, as depicted in Table 14-1.

Table 14-1. Thread states

Thread state	Description
NEW	A thread that is created but not started
RUNNABLE	A thread that is available to run
BLOCKED	An "alive" thread that is blocked waiting for a monitor lock
WAITING	An "alive" thread that calls its own wait() or join() while waiting on another thread

Thread state	Description
TIMED_WAITING	An "alive" thread that is waiting on another thread for a specified period of time; sleeping
TERMINATED	A thread that has completed

Thread Priorities

The valid range of priority values is typically 1 through 10, with a default value of 5. Thread priorities are one of the least portable aspects of Java, as their range and default values can vary among Java Virtual Machines (JVMs). Using MIN_PRIORITY, NORM_PRIOR ITY, and MAX_PRIORITY can retrieve priorities.

```
System.out.print(Thread.MAX_PRIORITY);
```

Lower priority threads yield to higher priority threads.

Common Methods

Table 14-2 contains common methods used for threads from the Thread class.

Table 14-2. Thread methods

Method	Description
getPriority()	Returns the thread's priority
getState()	Returns the thread's state
interrupt()	Interrupts the thread
isAlive()	Returns the thread's alive status
isInterrupted()	Checks for interruption of the thread
join()	Causes the thread to wait for another thread to complete
setPriority(int)	Sets the thread's priority
start()	Places the thread into a runnable state

Table 14-3 contains common methods used for threads from the Object class.

Table 14-3. Methods from the Object class used for threads

Method	Description
notify()	Tells a thread to wake up and run
notifyAll()	Tells all threads that are waiting on a thread or resource to wake up, and then the scheduler will select one of the threads to run
wait()	Pauses a thread in a wait state until another thread calls notify() or notifyAll()

TIP

Calls to wait() and notify() throw an InterruptedException if called on a thread that has its interrupted flag set to true.

Table 14-4 contains common static methods used for threads from the Thread class (i.e., Thread.sleep(1000)).

Table 14-4. Static thread methods

Method	Description
activeCount()	Returns number of threads in the current thread's group
currentThread()	Returns reference to the currently running thread
interrupted()	Checks for interruption of the currently running thread
sleep(long)	Blocks the currently running thread for *parameter* number of milliseconds
yield()	Pauses the current thread to allow other threads to run

Synchronization

The synchronized keyword provides a means to apply locks to blocks and methods. Locks should be applied to blocks and methods that access critically shared resources. These monitor locks begin and end with opening and closing braces. Following are some examples of synchronized blocks and methods.

Object instance t with a synchronized lock:

```
synchronized (t) {
  // Block body
}
```

Object instance this with a synchronized lock:

```
synchronized (this) {
  // Block body
}
```

Method raise() with a synchronized lock:

```
// Equivalent code segment 1
synchronized void raise() {
  // Method Body
}

// Equivalent code segment 2
void raise() {
  synchronized (this) {
    // Method body
  }
}
```

Static method calibrate() with a synchronized lock:

```
class Telescope {
  synchronized static void calibrate() {
    // Method body
  }
}
```

TIP

A lock is also known as a *monitor* or *mutex* (mutually exclusive lock).

The concurrent utilities provide additional means to apply and manage concurrency.

Concurrent Utilities

Java 2 SE 5.0 introduced utility classes for concurrent programming. These utilities reside in the `java.util.concurrent` package, and they include executors, concurrent collections, synchronizers, and timing utilities.

Executors

The class `ThreadPoolExecutor` as well as its subclass `Scheduled ThreadPoolExecutor` implement the `Executor` interface to provide configurable, flexible thread pools. Thread pools allow server components to take advantage of the reusability of threads.

The class `Executors` provides factory (object creator) methods and utility methods. Of them, the following are supplied to create thread pools:

`newCachedThreadPool()`
> Creates an unbounded thread pool that automatically reuses threads

`newFixedThreadPool(int nThreads)`
> Creates a fixed-size thread pool that automatically reuses threads off a shared unbounded queue

`newScheduledThreadPool(int corePoolSize)`
> Creates a thread pool that can have commands scheduled to run periodically or on a specified delay

`newSingleThreadExecutor()`
> Creates a single-threaded executor that operates off an unbounded queue

`newSingleThreadScheduledExecutor()`
> Creates a single-threaded executor that can have commands scheduled to run periodically or by a specified delay

The following example demonstrates usage of the `newFixed ThreadPool` factory method:

```
import java.util.concurrent.Executors;
import java.util.concurrent.ExecutorService;

public class ThreadPoolExample {
  public static void main() {
    // Create tasks
    // (from 'class RTask implements Runnable')
    RTask t1 = new RTask("thread1");
    RTask t2 = new RTask("thread2");

    // Create thread manager
    ExecutorService threadExecutor =
        Executors.newFixedThreadPool(2);

    // Make threads runnable
    threadExecutor.execute(t1);
    threadExecutor.execute(t2);

    // Shutdown threads
    threadExecutor.shutdown();
  }
}
```

Concurrent Collections

Even though collection types can be synchronized, it is best to use concurrent thread-safe classes that perform equivalent functionality, as represented in Table 14-5.

Table 14-5. Collections and their thread-safe equivalents

Collection class	Thread-safe equivalent
HashMap	ConcurrentHashMap
TreeMap	ConcurrentSkipListMap
TreeSet	ConcurrentSkipListSet
Map subtypes	ConcurrentMap
List subtypes	CopyOnWriteArrayList
Set subtypes	CopyOnWriteArraySet
PriorityQueue	PriorityBlockingQueue

Collection class	Thread-safe equivalent
Deque	BlockingDeque
Queue	BlockingQueue

Synchronizers

Synchronizers are special-purpose synchronization tools. Available synchronizers are listed in Table 14-6.

Table 14-6. Synchronizers

Synchronizer	Description
Semaphore	Maintains a set of permits
CountDownLatch	Implements waits against sets of operations being performed
CyclicBarrier	Implements waits against common barrier points
Exchanger	Implements a synchronization point where threads can exchange elements

Timing Utility

The TimeUnit enumeration is commonly used to inform time-based methods how a given timing parameter should be evaluated, as shown in the following example. Available TimeUnit enum constants are listed in Table 14-7.

```
// tyrLock (long time, TimeUnit unit)
if (lock.tryLock(15L, TimeUnit.DAYS)) {...} //15 days
```

Table 14-7. TimeUnit constants

Constants	Unit def.	Unit (sec)	Abbreviation
NANOSECONDS	1/1000 μs	.000000001	ns
MICROSECONDS	1/1000 ms	.000001	μs
MILLISECONDS	1/1000 sec	.001	ms
SECONDS	sec	1	sec
MINUTES	60 sec	60	min
HOURS	60 min	3600	hr
DAYS	24 hr	86400	d

CHAPTER 15

Java Collections Framework

The Java Collections Framework is designed to support numerous collections in a hierarchical fashion. It is essentially made up of interfaces, implementations, and algorithms.

The Collection Interface

Collections are objects that group multiple elements and store, retrieve, and manipulate those elements. The Collection interface is at the root of the collection hierarchy. Subinterfaces of Collection include List, Queue, and Set. Table 15-1 shows these interfaces and whether they are ordered or allow duplicates. The Map interface is also included in the table, as it is part of the framework.

Table 15-1. Common collections

Interface	Ordered	Dupes	Notes
List	Yes	Yes	Positional access; element insertion control
Map	Can be	No (Keys)	Unique keys; one value mapping max per key
Queue	Yes	Yes	Holds elements; usually FIFO
Set	Can be	No	Uniqueness matters

Implementations

Table 15-2 lists commonly used collection type implementations, their interfaces, and whether or not they are ordered, sorted, and/or contain duplicates.

Table 15-2. Collection type implementations

Implementations	Interface	Ordered	Sorted	Dupes	Notes
ArrayList	List	Index	No	Yes	Fast resizable array
LinkedList	List	Index	No	Yes	Doubly linked list
Vector	List	Index	No	Yes	Legacy, synchronized
HashMap	Map	No	No	No	Key/value pairs
Hashtable	Map	No	No	No	Legacy, synchronized
LinkedHash Map	Map	Insertion, last access	No	No	Linked list/hash table
TreeMap	Map	Balanced	Yes	No	Red-black tree map
Priority Queue	Queue	Priority	Yes	Yes	Heap implementation
HashSet	Set	No	No	No	Fast access set
LinkedHash Set	Set	Insertion	No	No	Linked list/hash set
TreeSet	Set	Sorted	Yes	No	Red-black tree set

Collection Framework Methods

The subinterfaces of the Collection interface provide several valuable method signatures, as shown in Table 15-3.

Table 15-3. Valuable subinterface methods

Method	List params	Set params	Map params	Returns
add	index, element	element	n/a	boolean
contains	Object	Object	n/a	boolean
containsKey	n/a	n/a	key	boolean
containsValue	n/a	n/a	value	boolean
get	index	n/a	key	Object
indexOf	Object	n/a	n/a	int
iterator	none	none	n/a	Iterator
keySet	n/a	n/a	none	Set
put	n/a	n/a	key, value	void
remove	index or Object	Object	key	void
size	none	none	none	int

Collections Class Algorithms

The Collections class, not to be confused with the Collection interface, contains several valuable static methods (i.e., algorithms). These methods can be invoked on a variety of collection types. Table 15-4 shows commonly used Collection class methods, their acceptable parameters, and return values.

Table 15-4. Collection class algorithms

Method	Parameters	Returns
addAll	Collection <? super T>, T...	boolean
max	Collection, [Comparator]	<T>
min	Collection, [Comparator]	<T>
disjoint	Collection, Collection	boolean
frequency	Collection, Object	int
asLifoQueue	Deque	Queue<T>
reverse	List	void

Method	Parameters	Returns
shuffle	List	void
copy	List destination, List source	void
rotate	List, int distance	void
swap	List, int position, int position	void
binarySearch	List, Object	int
fill	List, Object	void
sort	List, Object, [Comparator]	void
replaceAll	List, Object oldValue, Object newValue	boolean
newSetFromMap	Map	Set<E>

See Chapter 16 for more information on typed parameters (i.e., <T>).

Algorithm Efficiencies

Algorithms and data structures are optimized for different reasons—some for random element access, or insertion/deletion, others for keeping things in order. Depending on your needs, you may have to switch algorithms and structures.

Common collection algorithms, their types, and average time efficiencies are shown in Table 15-5.

Table 15-5. Algorithm efficiencies

Algorithms	Concrete type	Time
get, set	ArrayList	O(1)
add, remove	ArrayList	O(n)
contains, indexOf	ArrayList	O(n)
get, put, remove, constainsKey	HashMap	O(1)
add, remove, contains	HashSet	O(1)
add, remove, contains	LinkedHashSet	O(1)
get, set, add, remove (from either end)	LinkedList	O(1)

Algorithms	Concrete type	Time
get, set, add, remove (from index)	LinkedList	0 (n)
contains, indexOf	LinkedList	0 (n)
peek	PriorityQueue	0 (1)
add, remove	PriorityQueue	0 (log n)
remove, get, put, containsKey	TreeMap	0 (log n)
add, remove, contains	TreeSet	0 (log n)

The Big O notation is used to indicate time efficiencies, where *n* is the number of elements; see Table 15-6.

Table 15-6. Big O notation

Notation	Description
0 (1)	Time is constant, regardless of the number of elements.
0 (n)	Time is linear to the number of elements.
0 (log n)	Time is logarithmic to the number of elements.
0 (n log n)	Time is linearithmic to the number of elements.

Comparator Interface

Several methods in the Collections class assume that the objects in the collection are comparable. If there is no natural ordering, a helper class can implement the Comparator interface to specify how the objects are to be ordered:

```java
public class Crayon {
  private String color;
  public void setColor(String s)
  {color = s;}
  public String getColor()
  {return color;}
  public String toString()
  {return color;}
}

import java.util.Comparator;
```

```java
public class CrayonSort implements Comparator {
  public int compare (Crayon one, Crayon two) {
    return one.getColor().compareTo(two.getColor());
  }
}

import java.util.ArrayList;
import java.util.Collections;
public class ComparatorTest {
  public static void main(String[] args) {
    Crayon crayon1 = new Crayon();
    Crayon crayon2 = new Crayon();
    Crayon crayon3 = new Crayon();
    Crayon crayon4 = new Crayon();
    crayon1.setColor("green");
    crayon2.setColor("red");
    crayon3.setColor("blue");
    crayon4.setColor("purple");
    CrayonSort cSort = new CrayonSort();
    ArrayList cList = new
        ArrayList();
    cList.add(crayon1);
    cList.add(crayon2);
    cList.add(crayon3);
    cList.add(crayon4);
    Collections.sort(cList, cSort);
    System.out.println("\nSorted:" + cList );
  }
}

$ Sorted: [blue, green, purple, red]
```

CHAPTER 16

Generics Framework

The Generics Framework, introduced in Java SE 5.0, provides support that allows for the parameterization of types.

The benefit of generics is the significant reduction in the amount of code that needs to be written when developing a library. Another benefit is the elimination of casting in many situations.

The classes of the Collections Framework, the class Class, and other Java libraries have been updated to include generics.

See *Java Generics and Collections* by Maurice Naftalin and Philip Wadler (O'Reilly, 2006) for comprehensive coverage of the Generics Framework.

Generic Classes and Interfaces

Generic classes and interfaces parameterize types by adding a type parameter within angular brackets (i.e., <T>). The type is instantiated at the place of the brackets.

Once instantiated, the generic parameter type is applied throughout the class for methods that have the same type specified. In the following example, the add() and get() methods use the parameterized type as their parameter argument and return types, respectively:

```
public interface List <E> extends Collection<E>{
  public boolean add(E e);
  E get(int index);
}
```

When a variable of a parameterized type is declared, a concrete type (i.e., <Integer>) is specified to be used in place of the type parameter (i.e., <E>).

Subsequently, the need to cast when retrieving elements from things such as collections would be eliminated:

```
// Collection List/ArrayList with Generics
List<Integer> iList = new ArrayList<Integer>();
iList.add(1000);
// Explicit cast not necessary
Integer i = iList.get(0);

// Collection List/ArrayList without Generics
List iList = new ArrayList();
iList.add(1000);
// Explicit cast is necessary
Integer i = (Integer)iList.get(0);
```

The diamond operator <> was introduced in Java SE 7 to simplify the creation of generic types, by reducing the need for additional typing:

```
// Without the use of the diamond operator
List<Integer> iList1 = new ArrayList<Integer>();
// With the use of the diamond operator
List<Integer> iList2 = new ArrayList<>();
```

Constructors with Generics

Constructors of generic classes do not require generic type parameters as arguments:

```
// Generic Class
public class SpecialList <E> {
  // Constructor without arguments
  public SpecialList() {...}
```

```
    public SpecialList(String s) {...}
}
```

A generic object of this class could be instantiated as such:

```
SpecialList<String> b = new
        SpecialList<String>();
```

If a constructor for a generic class includes a parameter type such as a String, the generic object could be instantiated as such:

```
SpecialList<String> b = new
    SpecialList<String>("Joan Marie");
```

Substitution Principle

As specified in *Java Generics and Collections*, the Substitution Principle allows subtypes to be used where their supertype is parameterized:

- A variable of a given type may be assigned a value of any subtype of that type.

- A method with a parameter of a given type may be invoked with an argument of any subtype of that type.

Byte, Short, Integer, Long, Float, Double, BigInteger, and Big Decimal are all subtypes of class Number:

```
// List declared with generic Number type
List<Number> nList = new ArrayList<Number>();
nList.add((byte)27);      // Byte (Autoboxing)
nList.add((short)30000);  // Short
nList.add(1234567890);    // Integer
nList.add((long)2e62);    // Long
nList.add((float)3.4);    // Float
nList.add(4000.8);        // Double
nList.add(new BigInteger("9223372036854775810"));
nList.add(new BigDecimal("2.1e309"));

// Print Number's subtype values from the list
for( Number n : nList )
  System.out.println(n);
```

Type Parameters, Wildcards, and Bounds

The simplest declaration of a generic class is with an unbounded type parameter, such as T:

```
public class GenericClass <T> {...}
```

Bounds (constraints) and wildcards can be applied to the type parameter(s) as shown in Table 16-1.

Table 16-1. Type parameters, bounds, and wildcards

Type parameters	Description
`<T>`	Unbounded type; same as `<T extends Object>`
`<T,P>`	Unbounded types; `<T extends Object>` and `<P extends Object>`
`<T extends P>`	Upper bounded type; a specific type T that is a subtype of type P
`<T extends P & S>`	Upper bounded type; a specific type T that is a subtype of type P and that implements type S
`<T super P >`	Lower bounded type; a specific type T that is a supertype of type P
`<?>`	Unbounded wildcard; any object type, same as `<? extends Object>`
`<? extends P>`	Bounded wildcard; some unknown type that is a subtype of type P
`<? extends P & S>`	Bounded wildcard; some unknown type that is a subtype of type P and that implements type S
`<? super P>`	Lower bounded wildcard; some unknown type that is a supertype of type P

The Get and Put Principle

As also specified in *Java Generics and Collections*, the Get and Put Principle details the best usage of extends and super wildcards:

- Use an extends wildcard when you get only values out of a structure.

- Use a super wildcard when you put only values into a structure.

- Do not use a wildcard when you place both get and put values into a structure.

The extends wildcard has been used in the method declaration of the addAll() method of the List collection, as this method *gets* values from a collection:

```java
public interface List <E> extends Collection<E>{
  boolean addALL(Collection <? extends E> c)
}

List<Integer> srcList = new ArrayList<Integer>();
srcList.add(0);
srcList.add(1);
srcList.add(2);
// Using addAll() method with extends wildcard
List<Integer> destList = new ArrayList<Integer>();
destList.addAll(srcList);
```

The super wildcard has been used in the method declaration of the addAll() method of the class Collections, as the method *puts* values into a collection:

```java
public class Collections {
  public static <T> boolean addAll
      (Collection<? super T> c, T... elements){...}
}

// Using addAll() method with super wildcard
List<Number> sList = new ArrayList<Number>();
sList.add(0);
Collections.addAll(sList, (byte)1, (short)2);
```

Generic Specialization

A generic type can be extended in a variety of ways.

Given the parameterized abstract class `AbstractSet <E>`:

```
class SpecialSet<E> extends AbstractSet<E> {...}
```
> The `SpecialSet` class extends the `AbstractSet` class with the parameter type `E`. This is the typical way to declare generalizations with generics.

```
class SpecialSet extends AbstractSet<String> {...}
```
> The `SpecialSet` class extends the `AbstractSet` class with the parameterized type `String`.

```
class SpecialSet<E,P> extends AbstractSet<E> {...}
```
> The `SpecialSet` class extends the `AbstractSet` class with the parameter type `E`. Type `P` is unique to the `SpecialSet` class.

```
class SpecialSet<E> extends AbstractSet {...}
```
> The `SpecialSet` class is a generic class that would parameterize the generic type of the `AbstractSet` class. Because the raw type of the `AbstractSet` class has been extended (as opposed to generic), the parameterization cannot occur. Compiler warnings will be generated upon method invocation attempts.

```
class SpecialSet extends AbstractSet {...}
```
> The `SpecialSet` class extends the raw type of the `Abstract Set` class. Because the generic version of the `AbstractSet` class was expected, compiler warnings will be generated upon method invocation attempts.

Generic Methods in Raw Types

Static methods, nonstatic methods, and constructors that are part of nongeneric or raw type classes can be declared as generic. A raw type class is the nongeneric counterpart class to a generic class.

For generic methods of nongeneric classes, the method's return type must be preceded with the generic type parameter (i.e., <E>). However, there is no functional relationship between the type parameter and the return type, unless the return type is of the generic type:

```
public class SpecialQueue {
   public static <E> boolean add(E e) {...}
   public static <E> E peek() {...}
}
```

When calling the generic method, the generic type parameter is placed before the method name. Here, <String> is used to specify the generic type argument:

```
SpecialQueue.<String>add("White Carnation");
```

CHAPTER 17

The Java Scripting API

The Java Scripting API, introduced in Java SE 6, provides support that allows Java applications and scripting languages to interact through a standard interface. This API is detailed in JSR 223, "Scripting for the Java Platform" and is contained in the javax.script package.

Scripting Languages

Several scripting languages have script engine implementations available that conform to JSR 223. See "Scripting Languages (JSR-223 compatible)" on page 171 in Appendix A for a subset of these supported languages.

Script Engine Implementations

The ScriptEngine interface provides the fundamental methods for the API. The ScriptEngineManager class works in conjunction with this interface and provides a means to establish the desired scripting engines to be utilized.

Embedding Scripts into Java

The scripting API includes the ability to embed scripts and/or scripting components into Java applications.

The following example shows two ways to embed scripting components into a Java application: (1) the scripting engine's `eval` method reads in the scripting language syntax directly, and (2) the scripting engine's `eval` method reads the syntax in from a file.

```java
import java.io.FileReader;
import java.nio.file.Path;
import java.nio.file.Paths;
import javax.script.ScriptEngine;
import javax.script.ScriptEngineManager;

public class HelloWorld {
  public static void main(String[] args) throws
      Exception {
    ScriptEngineManager m
        = new ScriptEngineManager();
    // Sets up Rhino JavaScript Engine.
    ScriptEngine e = m.getEngineByExtension("js");
    // Rhino JavaScript syntax.
    e.eval("print ('Hello, ')");
    // world.js contents: print('World!\n');
    Path p1 = Paths.get("/opt/jpg2/world.js");
    e.eval(new FileReader(p1.toString()));
  }
}

$ Hello, World!
```

Invoking Methods of Scripting Languages

Scripting engines that implement the optional `Invocable` interface provide a means to invoke (execute) scripting language methods that the engine has already evaluated (interpreted).

The following Java-based `invokeFunction()` method calls the evaluated Rhino scripting language function `greet()`, which we have created:

```java
ScriptEngineManager m = new ScriptEngineManager();
ScriptEngine e = m.getEngineByExtension("js");
e.eval("function greet(message)
  + "{" + "println(message)" + "}");
```

```
Invocable i = (Invocable) e;
i.invokeFunction("greet", "Greetings from Mars!");

$ Greetings from Mars!
```

Accessing and Controlling Java Resources from Scripts

The Java Scripting API provides the ability to access and control Java resources (objects) from within evaluated scripting language code. The script engines utilizing key-value bindings is one way this is accomplished.

Here, the evaluated Rhino JavaScript makes use of the nameKey/ world binding and reads in (and prints out) a Java data member from the evaluated scripting language:

```
ScriptEngineManager m = new ScriptEngineManager();
ScriptEngine e = m.getEngineByExtension("js");
String world = "Gliese 581 c";
e.put("nameKey", world);
e.eval("var w = nameKey" );
e.eval("println(w)");

$ Gliese 581 c
```

By utilizing the key-value bindings, you can make modifications to the Java data members from the evaluated scripting language:

```
ScriptEngineManager m = new ScriptEngineManager();
ScriptEngine e = m.getEngineByExtension("js");
List<String> worldList = new ArrayList<>();
worldList.add ("Earth");
worldList.add ("Mars");
e.put("nameKey", worldList);
e.eval("var w = nameKey.toArray();");
e.eval(" nameKey.add (\"Gliese 581 c\")");
System.out.println(worldList);

$ [Earth, Gliese 581 c]
```

Setting Up Scripting Languages and Engines

Before using the Scripting API, you must obtain and set up the desired script engine implementations. Many scripting languages include the JSR-223 scripting engine with their distribution, either in a separate JAR or in their main JAR as in the case of JRuby.

Scripting Language Setup

Here are the steps for setting up the scripting language:

1. Set up the scripting language on your system. "Scripting Languages (JSR-223 compatible)" on page 171 in Appendix A contains a list of download sites for some supported scripting languages. Follow the associated installation instructions.

2. Invoke the script interpreters to ensure that they function properly. There is normally a command-line interpreter, as well as one with a graphical user interface.

For JRuby (as an example), the following commands should be validated to ensure proper setup:

```
jruby [file.rb] //Command line file
jruby.bat //Windows batch file
```

Scripting Engine Setup

Here are the steps for setting up the scripting engine:

1. Determine if your scripting language distribution includes the JSR-223 scripting API engine in its distribution. If it is included, steps 2 and 3 are not necessary.

2. Find and download the scripting engine file from the external resource (e.g., website).

3. Place the downloaded file into a directory and extract it to expose the necessary JAR. Note that the optional software (*opt*) directory is commonly used as an installation directory.

TIP

To install and configure certain scripting languages on a Windows machine, you may need a minimal POSIX-compliant shell, such as MSYS or Cygwin.

Scripting Engine Validation

Validate the scripting engine setup by compiling and/or interpreting the scripting language libraries and the scripting engine libraries. The following is an older version of JRuby where the engine was available externally:

```
javac -cp c:\opt\jruby-1.0\lib\jruby.jar;c:\opt\
jruby-engine.jar;. Engines
```

You can perform additional testing with short programs. The following application produces a list of the available scripting engine names, language version numbers, and extensions. Note that this updated version of JRuby includes JSR-223 support in its primary JAR file; therefore, the engine does not need to be separately called out on the class path:

```
$ java -cp c:\opt\jruby-1.6.7.2\lib\jruby.jar;.
EngineReport

import java.util.List;
import javax.script.ScriptEngineManager;
import javax.script.ScriptEngineFactory;

public class EngineReport {
  public static void main(String[] args) {
    ScriptEngineManager m =
```

```java
      new ScriptEngineManager();
    List<ScriptEngineFactory> s =
        m.getEngineFactories();
    // Iterate through list of factories
    for (ScriptEngineFactory f: s) {
      // Release name and version
      String en = f.getEngineName();
      String ev = f.getEngineVersion();
      System.out.println("Engine: "
        + en + " " + ev);
      // Language name and version
      String ln = f.getLanguageName();
      String lv = f.getLanguageVersion();
      System.out.println("Language: "
        + ln + " " + lv);
      // Extensions
      List<String> l = f.getExtensions();
      for (String x: l) {
        System.out.println("Extensions: " + x);
      }
    }
  }
}
```

```
$ Engine: Mozilla Rhino 1.7 release 3 PRERELEASE
$ Language: ECMAScript 1.8
$ Extensions: js

$ Engine: JSR 223 JRuby Engine 1.6.7.2
$ Language: ruby jruby 1.6.7.2
$ Extensions: rb
```

TIP

Rhino JavaScript is a scripting API packaged with Java SE and is available by default.

PART III
Appendixes

Third-Party Tools

A wide variety of open source and commercial third-party tools and technologies are available to assist you with developing Java-based applications.

The sample set of resources listed here are both effective and popular. Remember to check the licensing agreements of the open source tools you are using for commercial environment restrictions.

Development, CM, and Test Tools

Ant (http://bit.ly/16mhLiI)
> Ant is an XML-based tool for building and deploying Java applications. It's similar to the well-known Unix *make* utility.

Continuum (http://bit.ly/16mhLPB)
> Continuum is a continuous integration server that builds and tests code on a frequent, regular basis.

CruiseControl (http://bit.ly/16mhM6j)
> CruiseControl is a framework for a continuous build process. It includes a web interface to view build details and plug-ins for Ant, source control tools, and email notifications.

Enterprise Architect (http://bit.ly/16mhNqN)
> Enterprise Architect is a commercial Computer Aided Software Engineering (CASE) tool that provides forward and reverse Java code engineering with UML.

FindBugs (http://bit.ly/16mhMTO)
> FindBugs is a program that looks for bugs in Java code.

Git (http://bit.ly/16mhOep)
> Git is an open source distributed version control system.

Heatlamp (http://bit.ly/16mhQmD)
> Heatlamp renders clean, information-rich, interactive diagrams from live Java code.

Hudson (http://bit.ly/16mhPii)
> Hudson is an extensible continuous integration server.

Jalopy (http://bit.ly/16mhRGY)
> Jalopy is a source code formatter for Java that has plug-ins for Eclipse, jEdit, NetBeans, and other tools.

JDocs (http://bit.ly/16mhRXx)
> JDocs is a documentation repository that provides web access to Java API documentation of open source libraries.

jEdit (http://bit.ly/16mhTi5)
> jEdit is a text editor designed for programmers. It has several plug-ins available through a plug-in manager.

JavaFX SceneBuilder (http://bit.ly/16mhXOT)
> JavaFX Scene Builder is a visual layout tool for designing JavaFX applications.

Jenkins (http://bit.ly/XUeClg)
> Jenkins CI is an open source continuous integration server, formally known as "Hudson Labs."

JIRA (http://bit.ly/16mhVGM)
> JIRA is a commercial bug tracking, issue tracking, and project management application.

JMeter (http://bit.ly/16mhUCH)
    JMeter is an application that measures system behavior, such as functional behavior and performance.

JUnit (http://bit.ly/16mhWdY)
    JUnit is a framework for unit testing that provides a means to write and run repeatable tests.

Maven (http://bit.ly/16mhV9O)
    Maven is a software project management tool for enterprise Java projects. Maven can manage builds, reports, and documentation.

Nemo (http://bit.ly/16mhYm2)
    Nemo is an online instance of Sonar dedicated to open source projects.

PMD (http://bit.ly/16mhY5z)
    PMD scans Java source code for bugs, suboptimal code, and overly complicated expressions.

Sonar (http://bit.ly/16mhZ9B)
    Sonar is an open source quality management platform.

Subversion (http://bit.ly/16mhZq9)
    Subversion is a centralized version control system that keeps track of work and changes for a set of files.

Libraries

ActiveMQ (http://bit.ly/16mhZWY)
    ActiveMQ is a message broker that supports many cross-language clients and protocols.

BIRT (http://bit.ly/16mi0dz)
    BIRT is an open source Eclipse-based reporting system to be used with Java EE applications.

Hibernate (http://bit.ly/16mi2Ck)
    Hibernate is an object/relational persistence and query service. It allows for the development of persistent classes.

iText (http://bit.ly/16mi3Gp)
> iText is a Java library that allows for the creation and manipulation of PDF documents.

Jackrabbit (http://bit.ly/16mi4da)
> Jackrabbit is a content repository system that provides hierarchical content storage and control.

Jakarta Commons (http://bit.ly/16mi4tM)
> Jakarta Commons is a repository of reusable Java components.

Jasper Reports (http://bit.ly/16mi6Sy)
> Jasper Reports is an open source Java reporting engine.

Jasypt (http://bit.ly/16mi796)
> Jasypt is a Java library that allows the developer to add basic encryption capabilities.

JFreeChart (http://bit.ly/16mi5hq)
> JFreeChart is a Java class library for generating charts.

JFXtras2 (http://bit.ly/16mi5Oy)
> JFXtras2 is a set of controls and add-ons for JavaFX 2.0.

JGoodies (http://bit.ly/16mi90J)
> JGoodies provides components and solutions to solve common user interface tasks.

JIDE (http://bit.ly/16mi5Oh)
> JIDE software provides various Java and Swing components.

JMonkeyEngine (http://bit.ly/16mi9xy)
> JMonkeyEngine is a collection of libraries providing a Java 3D (OpenGL) game engine.

JOGL (http://bit.ly/16micto)
> JOGL is a Java API supporting OpenGL and ES specifications.

RXTX (http://bit.ly/16mid0f)
> RXTX provides native serial and parallel communications for Java.

Spring Framework (http://bit.ly/16midgS)
> The Spring Framework is a layered Java/Java EE application framework.

Integrated Development Environments

BlueJ (http://bit.ly/16migJu)
> BlueJ is an IDE designed for introductory teaching.

Eclipse IDE (http://bit.ly/16mih05)
> Eclipse IDE is an IDE for creating Java applets and applications.

IntelliJ IDEA (http://bit.ly/16miel3)
> IntelliJ IDEA is a commercial IDE for creating Java applets and applications.

JBuilder (http://bit.ly/16mihxd)
> JBuilder is a commercial IDE for creating Java applets and applications.

JCreator (http://bit.ly/16mihNJ)
> JCreator is a commercial IDE for creating Java applets and applications.

JDeveloper (http://bit.ly/15XCBkv)
> JDeveloper is Oracle's IDE for creating Java applets and applications.

NetBeans (http://bit.ly/16miikG)
> NetBeans is Oracle's open source IDE for creating Java applets and applications.

Web Application Platforms

Geronimo (http://bit.ly/16miiBc)

Geronimo is a Java EE server used for developing, integrating, and deploying applications, portals, and web services.

Glassfish (http://bit.ly/16migcz)

Glassfish is an open source Java EE server used for developing, integrating, and deploying applications, portals, and web services.

IBM WebSphere (http://ibm.co/16mij8l)

IBM WebSphere is a commercial Java EE server used for developing, integrating, and deploying applications, portals, and web services.

JavaServer Faces (http://bit.ly/16mimkj)

JavaServer Faces technology simplifies building user interfaces for JavaServer applications. JSF implementations include Apache MyFaces, ICEFaces, RichFaces, and Primefaces.

Jetty (http://bit.ly/16miksP)

Jetty is a web container for Java Servlets and JavaServer Pages.

Oracle WebLogic Application Server (http://bit.ly/16mikZM)

Oracle WebLogic Application Server is a commercial Java EE server used for developing, integrating, and deploying applications, portals, and web services.

Resin (http://bit.ly/16milgv)

Resin is a high-performance, cloud-optimized Java application server.

Seam Framework (http://bit.ly/16milNe)

Seam Framework is an open source web development platform.

ServiceMix (http://bit.ly/16mioc4)

ServiceMix is an enterprise service bus that combines the functionality of a service-oriented architecture and an event-driven architecture on the Java Business Integration specification.

Sling (http://bit.ly/16mioZF)

Sling is a web application framework that leverages off of the Representational State Transfer (REST) software architecture style.

Struts (http://bit.ly/16mipwx)

Struts is a framework for creating enterprise-ready Java web applications that utilize a model-view-controller architecture.

Tapestry (http://bit.ly/16miq3x)

Tapestry is a framework for creating web applications based upon the Java Servlet API.

Tomcat (http://bit.ly/16misIJ)

Tomcat is a web container for Java Servlets and JavaServer Pages.

WildFly (http://bit.ly/16mimB0)

WildFly, formally known as JBoss Application Server, is an open source Java EE server used for developing, integrating, and deploying applications, portals, and web services.

Scripting Languages (JSR-223 compatible)

BeanShell (http://bit.ly/16mitfM)

BeanShell is an embeddable Java source interpreter with object-based scripting language features.

Clojure (http://bit.ly/16miwIo)

Clojure is a dynamic programming language targeted for the Java Virtual Machine, Common Language Runtime, and JavaScript engines.

FreeMarker (http://bit.ly/16miwZa)

FreeMarker is a Java-based general-purpose template engine.

Groovy (http://bit.ly/16mivo0)

Groovy is a scripting language with many Python, Ruby, and Smalltalk features in a Java-like syntax.

Jacl (http://bit.ly/16miws2)

Jacl is a pure Java implementation of the Tcl scripting language.

JEP (http://bit.ly/16mixMz)

Java Math Expression Parser (JEP) is a Java library for parsing and evaluating mathematical expressions.

Jawk (http://bit.ly/16miz7h)

Jawk is a pure Java implementation of the AWK scripting language.

Jelly (http://bit.ly/16miD6O)

Jelly is a scripting tool used for turning XML into executable code.

JRuby (http://bit.ly/16miEHY)

JRuby is a pure Java implementation of the Ruby programming language.

Jython (http://bit.ly/16miG2B)

Jython is a pure Java implementation of the Python programming language.

Rhino (http://mzl.la/16miGzy)

Rhino is a JavaScript implementation. It is the *only* scripting language that has a script engine implementation included in the Java Scripting API by default.

Scala (http://bit.ly/16miGQf)

Scala is a general-purpose programming language designed to express common programming patterns in a concise, elegant, and type-safe way.

Sleep (http://bit.ly/16miIY9)

Sleep, based on Perl, is an embeddable scripting language for Java applications.

Visage (http://bit.ly/16miJeF)

Visage is a domain specific language (DSL) designed for the express purpose of writing user interfaces.

Velocity (http://bit.ly/16miKzh)

Velocity is a Java-based general-purpose template engine.

UML Basics

Unified Modeling Language (UML) is an object modeling specification language that uses graphical notation to create an abstract model of a system. The Object Management Group (*http://bit.ly/16miJLR*) governs UML. This modeling language can be applied to Java programs to help graphically depict such things as class relationships and sequence diagrams. The latest specifications for UML can be found at the OMG website (*http://bit.ly/16miLmZ*). An informative book on UML is *UML Distilled*, Third Edition, by Martin Fowler (Addison-Wesley, 2003).

Class Diagrams

A class diagram represents the static structure of a system, displaying information for classes and relationships between them. The individual class diagram is divided into three compartments: name, attributes (optional), and operations (optional); see Figure B-1 and the example that follows it.

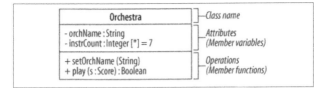

Figure B-1. Class diagram

```
// Corresponding code segment
class Orchestra { // Class Name
  // Attributes
  private String orch Name;
  private Integer instrCount = 7;
  // Operations
  public void setOrchName(String name) {...}
  public Boolean play(Score s) {...}
}
```

Name

The name compartment is required and includes the class or interface name typed in boldface.

Attributes

The attributes compartment is optional and includes member variables that represent the state of the object. The complete UML usage is as follows:

```
visibility name : type [multiplicity] = defaultValue
{property-string}
```

Typically, only the attribute names and types are represented.

Operations

The operations compartment is optional and includes member functions that represent the system's behavior. The complete UML usage for operations is as follows:

```
visibility name (parameter-list) :
return-type-expression
{property-string}
```

Typically, only the operation names and parameter lists are represented.

TIP

{property-string} can be any of several properties such as
{ordered} or {read-only}.

Visibility

Visibility indicators (prefix symbols) can be optionally defined
for access modifiers. The indicators can be applied to the member
variables and member functions of a class diagram; see Table B-1.

Table B-1. Visibility indicators

Visibility indicators	Access modifiers
~	*package-private*
#	protected
-	private
+	

Object Diagrams

Object diagrams are differentiated from class diagrams by underlining the text in the object's name compartment. The text can
be represented three different ways; see Table B-2.

Table B-2. Object names

: ClassName	Class name only
objectName	Object name only
objectName : ClassName	Object and class name

Object diagrams are not frequently used, but they can be helpful when detailing information, as shown in Figure B-2.

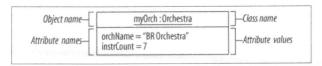

Figure B-2. Object diagram

Graphical Icon Representation

Graphical icons are the main building blocks in UML diagrams; see Figure B-3.

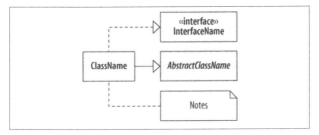

Figure B-3. Graphical icon representation

Classes, Abstract Classes, and Interfaces

Classes, abstract classes, and interfaces are all represented with their names in boldface within a rectangle. Abstract classes are additionally italicized. Interfaces are prefaced with the word *interface* enclosed in guillemet characters. Guillemets house stereotypes and in the interface case, a classifier.

Notes

Notes are comments in a rectangle with a folded corner. They can be represented alone, or they can be connected to another icon by a dashed line.

Packages

A package is represented with an icon that resembles a file folder. The package name is inside the larger compartment unless the larger compartment is occupied by other graphical elements (i.e., class icons). In the latter case, the package name would be in the smaller compartment. An open arrowhead with a dashed line shows package dependencies.

The arrow always points in the direction of the package that is required to satisfy the dependency. Package diagrams are shown in Figure B-4.

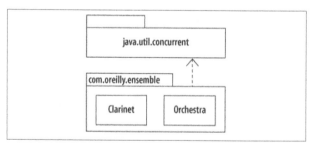

Figure B-4. Package diagrams

Connectors

Connectors are the graphical images that show associations between classes. Connectors are detailed in "Class Relationships" on page 181.

Multiplicity Indicators

Multiplicity indicators represent how many objects are participating in an association; see Table B-3. These indicators are typically included next to a connector and can also be used as part of a member variable in the attributes compartment.

Table B-3. Multiplicity indicators

Indicator	Definition
*	Zero or more objects
0..*	Zero or more objects
0..1	Optional (zero or one object)
0..n	Zero to n objects where $n > 1$
1	Exactly one object
1..*	One or more objects
1..n	One to n objects where $n > 1$
m..n	Specified range of objects
n	Only n objects where $n > 1$

Role Names

Role names are utilized when the relationships between classes need to be further clarified. Role names are often seen with multiplicity indicators. Figure B-5 shows Orchestra where it *performs* one or more Scores.

Figure B-5. Role names

Class Relationships

Class relationships are represented by the use of connectors and class diagrams; see Figure B-6. Graphical icons, multiplicity indicators, and role names may also be used in depicting relationships.

Association

An association denotes a relationship between classes and can be bidirectionally implied. Class attributes and multiplicities can be included at the target end(s).

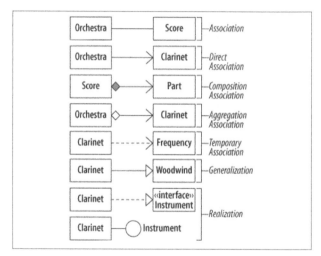

Figure B-6. Class relationships

Direct Association

Direct association, also known as navigability, is a relationship directing the source class to the target class. This relationship may be read Orchestra "has-a" Clarinet. Class attributes and multiplicities can be included at the target end. Navigability can be bidirectional between classes.

Composition Association

Composition association, also known as *containment*, models a whole-part relationship, where the whole governs the lifetime of the parts. The parts cannot exist except as components of the whole. This is a stronger form of association than aggregation. You could say a Score is "composed-of" one or more part(s).

Aggregation Association

Aggregation association models a whole-part relationship where the parts may exist independently of the whole. The whole does not govern the existence of the parts. You could say Orchestra is the whole and Clarinet is "part-of" Orchestra.

Temporary Association

Temporary association, better known as *dependency*, is represented where one class requires the existence of another class. It's also seen in cases where an object is used as a local variable, return value, or a member function argument. Passing a frequency to a tune method of class Clarinet can be read as class Clarinet depends on class Frequency, or Clarinet "uses-a" Frequency.

Generalization

Generalization is where a specialized class inherits elements of a more general class. In Java, we know this as inheritance, such as class extends class Woodwind, or Clarinet "is-a(n)" Woodwind.

Realization

Realization models a class implementing an interface, such as class Clarinet implements interface Instrument.

Sequence Diagrams

UML sequence diagrams are used to show dynamic interaction between objects; see Figure B-7. The collaboration starts at the top of the diagram and works its way toward the bottom.

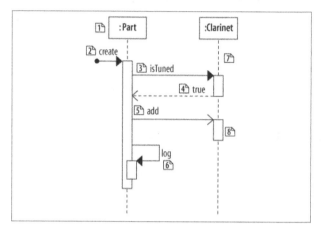

Figure B-7. Sequence diagrams

Participant (1)

The participants are considered objects.

Found Message (2)

A found message is one in which the caller is not represented in the diagram. This means that the sender is not known, or does not need to be shown in the given diagram.

Synchronous Message (3)

A synchronous message is used when the source waits until the target has finished processing the message.

Return Call (4)

The return call can optionally depict the return value and is typically excluded from sequence diagrams.

Asynchronous Message (5)

An asynchronous message is used when the source does not wait
for the target to finish processing the message.

Message to Self (6)

A message to self, or *self-call*, is defined by a message that stays
within the object.

Lifeline (7)

Lifelines are associated with each object and are oriented verti-
cally. They are related to time and are read downward, with the
earliest event at the top of the page.

Activation Bar (8)

The activation bar is represented on the lifeline or another activation bar. The bar shows when the participant (object) is active
in the collaboration.

Index

Symbols

@Deprecated annotation, 53
@Override annotation, 53
@SuppressWarnings annotation, 53

A

abstract classes, 49
    graphical icon representations in UML, 178
abstract keyword, 49
abstract methods, 49
abstract modifier, 79, 81
Abstract Window Toolkit (AWT) API, 90
AbstractSet <E> parameterized abstract class, extending, 154
access modifiers, 80, 177
    overloaded methods, 43
    overridden methods, 44
    subclasses' access to superclass members, 46
accessor methods, 42

acronyms in names, 6
annotations, 53–54
    built-in, 53
    developer-defined, 54
anonymous arrays, 32
API libraries, 86–97
    base, 87
    integration, 89
    language and utility, 86
    Remote Method Invocation (RMI) and CORBA, 93
    security, 94
    user interface
        Abstract Window Toolkit (AWT), 90
        miscellaneous, 90
        Swing, 91
    XML, 95
ArithmeticException, 68
ArrayIndexOutOfBoundsException, 68
ArrayList class, 144
    algorithm efficiencies, 146

We'd like to hear your suggestions for improving our indexes. Send email to index@oreilly.com.

arrays
  default values, 31
  of primitives, 27
ASCII
  nonprintable characters, 9
  printable characters, 8
AssertionError, 69
assertions, 62
ATOMIC_MOVE, 131
autoboxing, 26
Autoclosable interface, 74
AWT (Abstract Window Toolkit)
  API, 90

B

base libraries, 87
Big O notation (time efficiencies),
  147
binary data
  reading from files, 122
  reading from sockets, 123
  writing to files, 123
  writing to sockets, 124
binary numeric promotion (primitive types), 24
BLOCKED (thread state), 134
blocks, 56
Boolean literals, 13
bounds, applied to type parameters, 152
break statement, 58, 60
BufferedInputStream class, 122,
  124
BufferedOutputStream class, 123,
  124
BufferedReader class, 121, 123

C

case statement, 58
catch blocks
  multi-catch clause, 74
  try-catch statement, 71
  try-catch-finally statement, 73

catch keyword, 70
character data
  reading from files, 121
  reading from sockets, 123
  writing to files, 122
  writing to sockets, 124
character literals, 14
Character.isJavaIdentifierStart( )
  method, 11
checked exceptions, 66
  common, 67
class diagrams, 175–177
  attributes, 176
  name, 176
  operations, 176
  visibility indicators, 177
class names, 3
class relationships (UML), 181
  association, 181
    aggregation association,
      182
    composition association,
      182
    direct association, 182
    temporary association, 182
  generalization, 182
  realization, 182
ClassCastException, 68
classes, 41–48
  abstract, 49, 81
  calling constructor from an-
    other constructor in same
    class, 47
  constructors, 45
  data members and methods,
    42
  defined, 41
  enum, 52
  final, 81
  generic, 149
  graphical icon representations
    in UML, 178
  implementing an interface, 52

input and output, hierarchy, 120
instantiating, 42
local, 56
nongeneric, generic methods of, 155
static constants, 51
static data members, 50
static initializers, 51
static methods, 50
strictfp, 81
syntax, 42
ClassNotFoundException, 67
classpath, 109
CLASSPATH environment variable, 110
CloneNotSupportedException, 68
cloning objects, 38
shallow and deep cloning, 39
CM tools, 165
collections
and thread-safe equivalents, 139
defined, 143
generic types, 150
Collections Framework, 143–148
algorithm efficiencies, 146
Collection interface, 143
collection type implementations, 144
Collections class algorithms, 145
Comparator interface, 147
generic type parameter names, 5
subinterfaces of Collection, methods, 144
command-line tools, 102–109
JAR file execution, 106
Java compiler, 102
Java interpreter, 104
Java program packager, 106
javadoc, 108

comments, 9
Javadoc, 108
Comparator interface, 147
compiler, 102
compression
compressing and uncompressing GZIP files, 126
creating ZIP and GZIP files, 126
concurrency, 133–141
common methods, 135
from Object class, 135
from Thread class, 135
static Thread class methods, 136
concurrent utilities, 138
concurrent collections, 139
executors, 138
synchronizers, 140
timing utility, 140
creating threads, 133
extending Thread class, 133
implementing Runnable interface, 134
synchronization, 136
thread priorities, 135
thread states, 134
concurrent mark-sweep (CMS) garbage collector, 113
conditional operators (? :), special cases for, 25
conditional statements, 56–58
if, 56
if else, 57
if else if, 57
switch, 58
constant names, 5
constants
accessing with dot operator (.), 50
static, 51

constructors, 45
    calling using this keyword, 47
    enum classes, 52
    superclass, calling, 46
    with generics, 150
containment, 182
continue statement, 61
conversions
    between primitives and reference types, 33
    of reference types, 32
COPY_ATTRIBUTES, 131
CORBA libraries, 94
currency symbols, 17

D

data members, 42
    accessing in objects, 43
    enum classes, 52
    final, 81
    static, 50, 81
    superclass, subclass's access to, 46
    transient, 82, 125
    volatile, 82
DataInputStream class, 122, 123, 124
DataOutputStream class, 123
debugging, using assertions, 62
deep cloning, 39
@Deprecated annotation, 53
deserialization, 125
development, 99–110
    classpath, 109
    command-line tools, 102–109
        JAR file execution, 106
        Java compiler, 102
        Java documenter, 108
        Java interpreter, 104
        Java program packager, 106
        Java program structure, 100

        JDK (Java Development Kit), 100
        JRE (Java Runtime Environment), 99
        third-party tools, 165
diamond operator <>, 150
directories, 121
    (see also files and directories)
directory structure, on different operating systems, 109
do while loop, 60
documentation, javadoc command-line tool, 108
dot operator (.)
    accessing data members and methods in objects, 43
    accessing static data members, methods, constants and initializers, 50
Double class, methods to determine if number is infinite or NaN, 22

E

empty statement, 56
encapsulation, 42
enumerations, 52
    comparing, 37
    names, 5
EOFException, 68
equality operator (==), 35–37
equals( ) method, 35
err stream, 120
Error class, 75
errors, 67
    common, 69
escape sequences, 16
Exception class, 66, 75
exception handling, 65–77
    checked exceptions, 66
    common checked exceptions, 67
    common errors, 69

common unchecked exceptions, 68
defining your own exception class, 75
errors, 67
exception hierarchy, 65
keywords, 69–74
    multi-catch clause, 74
    throw, 70
    try-catch statement, 71
    try-catch-finally statement, 73
    try-finally statement, 72
    try-with-resources statement, 73
    try/catch/finally, 70
printing information about exceptions, 76
    getMessage( ) method, 76
    printStackTrace( ) method, 76
    toString( ) method, 76
steps in process, 74
unchecked exceptions, 66
exception handling statements, 63
ExceptionInitializeError, 69
exceptions, defined, 65
Executor interface, 138
Executors class, methods producing thread pools, 138
explicit garbage collection, 118
expression statements, 55
extends keyword, 46
extends wildcard, 152

F

fields, 42
FileNotFoundException, 68
FileReader class, 121
files and directories
    file reading and writing, 121–123
    handling, 127
        commonly used methods in File class, 127
    zipping and unzipping files, 126
Files class, 130
FileVisitor interface, 131
FileWriter class, 122
final modifier, 79, 81
finalize( ) method, 118
finally blocks
    try-catch-finally statement, 73
    try-finally statement, 72
finally keyword, 70
Float class, methods to determine if number is infinite or NaN, 22
floating-point entities, 21
    operations involving, 23
floating-point literals, 15
for each loop, 59
for in loop, 59
for loop, 59
    enhanced, 59
fundamental types, 19–28

G

garbage collection (GC), 111
    explicit, 118
    finalization, 118
    garbage collectors, 111
    GC related command-line options for Java interpreter, 114
    reference types, 39
Garbage-First (G1) collector, 113
GC (see garbage collection)
Generics Framework, 149–155
    constructors with generics, 150
    generic classes and interfaces, 149
    generic methods in raw types, 154

generic specialization, 154
generic type parameter names, 4
Get and Put Principle, 152
Substitution Principle, 151
type parameters, wildcards, and bounds, 152
Get and Put Principle, 152
getMessage( ) method, 76
GZIP files, 126
    compressing and uncompressing, 126

H

hashCode( ) method, 35
HashMap class, 144
    algorithm efficiencies, 146
HashSet class, 144
    algorithm efficiencies, 146
Hashtable class, 144
heap
    object references with value of null and, 31
    resizing JVM heap, 117
HPROF (Heap/CPU Profiling Tool), 113

I

identifiers, 11
IDEs (Integrated Development Environments), 100, 169
IEEE 754-1985 standard (floating-point entities), 21
if else if statement, 57
if else statement, 57
if statement, 56
IllegalArgumentException, 68
IllegalStateException, 68
immutability, 42
implements keyword, 52
import statements, 101
in stream, 119
IndexOutOfBoundsException, 69

Infinity, 21
-Infinity (negative infinity), 22
inheritance, 41
    overriding inherited methods, 44
    superclasses and subclasses, 46
initializers, static, 51
input and output, 119–128
    class hierarchy, 120
    file and directory handling, 127
        accessing existing files, 127
        File class, commonly used methods, 127
        seeking in files, 128
    file reading and writing, 121–123
        reading binary data from a file, 122
        reading character data from a file, 121
        writing binary data to a file, 123
        writing character data to a file, 122
    NIO 2.0 (see NIO 2.0)
    serialization, 125
        deserializing an object, 125
        serializing an object, 125
    socket reading and writing, 123
        binary data to a socket, 124
        reading binary data from a socket, 123
        reading character data from a socket, 123
        writing character data to a socket, 124
    standard streams in, out, and err, 119

zipping and unzipping files, 126
    compressing and uncompressing GZIP files, 126
input and output streams, 120
InputStream class, 122
instance variable names, 4
instance variables, 42
    default value, 30
integer literals, 14
Integrated Development Environments (IDEs), 100, 169
integration libraries, 89
interface keyword, 51
interface names, 3
interfaces, 51
    generic, 149
    graphical icon representations in UML, 178
interpreter, 104
    GC related command-line options for, 114
InterruptedException, 68, 136
IOException, 68, 119
iteration statements, 58–60
    do while loop, 60
    for loop, 59
        enhanced, 59
    while loop, 59

J

JAR (Java Archive) files, 106
    execution, 106
Java Archive (JAR) utility, 106
Java Collections Framework (see Collections Framework)
Java Development Kit (see JDK)
Java HotSpot VM options, 114
Java interpreter, 104
Java modifiers (see modifiers)
Java Platform, SE (Standard Edition), 85

Java Programming Language, 85
Java Runtime Environment (see JRE)
Java Scripting API, 157–162
    script engine implementations, 157
        accessing and controlling Java resources from scripts, 159
        embedding scripts into Java, 157
        invoking methods of scripting languages, 158
    scripting languages, 157
    setting up scripting languages and engines, 160
        scripting engine setup, 160
        scripting engine validation, 161
        scripting language setup, 160
Java Virtual Machines (see JVMs)
java.applet, 87
java.awt, 90
java.awt.color, 91
java.awt.datatransfer, 91
java.awt.dnd, 91
java.awt.event, 91
java.awt.font, 91
java.awt.geom, 91
java.awt.im, 91
java.awt.image, 91
java.awt.image.renderable, 91
java.awt.print, 91
java.beans, 87
java.io, 87
java.lang, 86, 101
java.lang.annotation, 86
java.lang.instrument, 86
java.lang.invoke, 86
java.lang.management, 86
java.lang.ref, 86

java.math, 88
java.net, 88
    Socket class, 123
java.nio, 88
java.nio.channels, 88
java.nio.charset, 88
java.nio.file, 88
java.nio.file.attribute, 88
java.rmi, 93
java.rmi.activation, 93
java.rmi.dgc, 93
java.rmi.registry, 93
java.rmi.server, 93
java.security.cert, 94
java.security.interfaces, 94
java.security.spec, 94
java.sql, 89
java.text, 88
java.util, 86, 101
java.util.concurrent, 87, 138
java.util.concurrent.atomic, 87
java.util.concurrent.locks, 87
java.util.jar, 87
java.util.logging, 87
java.util.prefs, 87
java.util.regex, 87
java.util.zip, 87
javac compiler, 102
javadoc, 108
Javadoc comments, 10
JavaFX Runtime libraries, 86
javaw interpreter, 105
javax.accessibility, 90
javax.annotation, 88
javax.crypto, 94
javax.crypto.interfaces, 94
javax.crypto.spec, 95
javax.imageio, 90
javax.jws.soap, 89, 89
javax.management, 88
javax.naming, 89
javax.naming.directory, 89
javax.naming.event, 89

javax.naming.ldap, 89
javax.net, 88
javax.net.ssl, 88
javax.print, 90
javax.print.attribute, 90
javax.print.attribute.standard, 90
javax.print.event, 90
javax.rmi, 94
javax.rmi.CORBA, 94
javax.rmi.ssl, 94
javax.script, 89, 157
javax.security.auth, 95
javax.security.auth.callback, 95
javax.security.auth.kerberos, 95
javax.security.auth.login, 95
javax.security.auth.x500, 95
javax.security.sasl, 95
javax.sound.midi, 90
javax.sound.sampled, 90
javax.sql, 89
javax.sql.rowset, 89
javax.sql.rowset.serial, 89
javax.swing, 91
javax.swing.border, 92
javax.swing.colorchooser, 92
javax.swing.event, 92
javax.swing.filechooser, 92
javax.swing.plaf, 92
javax.swing.plaf.basic, 92
javax.swing.plaf.metal, 92
javax.swing.plaf.multi, 92
javax.swing.plaf.nimbus, 92
javax.swing.plaf.synth, 92
javax.swing.table, 92
javax.swing.text, 92
javax.swing.text.html, 93
javax.swing.text.html.parser, 93
javax.swing.text.rtf, 93
javax.swing.tree, 93
javax.swing.undo, 93
javax.tools, 88
javax.transactions.xa, 90
javax.xml, 95

javax.xml.bind, 95
javax.xml.crypto, 96
javax.xml.crypto.dom, 96
javax.xml.crypto.dsig, 96
javax.xml.datatype, 96
javax.xml.namespace, 96
javax.xml.parsers, 96
javax.xml.soap, 96
javax.xml.transform, 96
javax.xml.transform.dom, 96
javax.xml.transform.sax, 96
javax.xml.transform.stax, 96
javax.xml.validation, 96
javax.xml.ws, 96
javax.xml.ws.handler, 97
javax.xml.ws.handler.soap, 97
javax.xml.ws.http, 97
javax.xml.ws.soap, 97
javax.xml.xpath, 97
jconsole tool, 113
jdb (Java debugger) tool, 113
JDK (Java Development Kit), 85,
    100
    memory management tools,
        113
jhat tool, 113
jinfo tool, 113
jmap tool, 113
JRE (Java Runtime Environment),
    85, 99
JRuby
    setup, 160
    validation of scripting engine
        setup, 161
jstack tool, 113
jstat tool, 113
jvisualvm tool, 113
JVMs (Java Virtual Machines), 85,
    99
    GC related options for inter-
        preter's interaction with
        Java HotSpot VM, 114
    resizing JVM heap, 117

thread priorities, variations in,
    135

K

key-value bindings, script engines
    utilizing, 159
keywords, 10

L

labels, loops or statements, 61
language and utility libraries, 86
libraries, 86
    (see also API libraries)
    third-party, 167
line terminators, 17
LinkedHashMap class, 144
LinkedHashSet class, 144, 146
LinkedList class, 144, 146
List interface, 143
    methods, 144
literals, 13
    Boolean, 13
    character, 14
    floating-point, 15
    for primitive types, 20
    integer, 14
    null, 16
    string, 15
local classes, 56
local variable names, 4
local variables, 56
    no default value, 31
locks, 136

M

main( ) method, 102
manifest file, 107
Map interface, 143
    methods, 144
marker annotations, 54
MAX_PRIORITY (threads), 135
memory allocation, reference
    types, 39

memory management, 111–118
  garbage collectors, 111
  GC related command-line options for Java interpreter interfacing with Java Hot-Spot VM, 114
  interfacing with the garbage collector, 118
    explicit garbage collection, 118
    finalization, 118
  resizing JVM heap, 117
  tools for, 113
metadata, association with program elements through annotations, 53
method names, 4
methods, 42
  abstract, 49, 81
  accessing in objects, 43
  Collection Framework, 144
  enum classes, 52
  final, 81
  generic methods in raw types, 154
  interface, 51
  native, 81
  overloading, 43
  overriding, 44
  passing reference types into, 33
  static, 50, 81
  strictfp, 81
  synchronized, 82
    raise( ) method with synchronized lock, 137
  variable-length argument lists (varargs), 48
MIN_PRIORITY (threads), 135
modifiers, 79–82
  access, 80
  other (nonaccess), 81
monitor, 137
multi-catch clause, 74

multidimensional arrays, 32
multiline comments, 9
multivalue annotations, 54
mutator methods, 42
mutex, 137

N

naming conventions, 3–6
  acronyms, 6
  class names, 3
  constant names, 5
  generic type parameter names, 4
  instance and static variable names, 4
  interface names, 3, 51
  method names, 4
  package names, 5
  parameter and local variable names, 4
Nan (Not-a-Number), 21
narrowing conversions, 33
native modifier, 79, 81
navigability, 182
negative infinity (-Infinity), 22
negative zero (-0), 21
NEW (thread state), 134
new keyword, creating objects, 42
newFixedThreadPool( ) method, Executors class, 138
newline variations, 17
NIO (new I/O) APIs, 119
NIO 2.0, 129–131
  additional features, 131
  Files class, 130
  Path interface, 129
NoClassDefFoundError, 69
NOFOLLOW_LINKS, 131
NORM_PRIORITY (threads), 135
NoSuchMethodException, 68
not equal (!=) operator, 35
Not-a-Number (see NaN)
null literals, 16

NullPointerException, 31, 69
NumberFormatException, 69

O

Object class, 29
    equals( ) method, 35
    methods used for threads, 135
object diagrams, 177
object instances with synchronized
        lock, 137
object-oriented programming
        (OOP), 41–54
    abstract classes and abstract
            methods, 49
    annotations, 53–54
        built-in, 53
        developer-defined, 54
    classes and objects, 41–48
    enumerations, 52
    interfaces, 51
    static constants, 51
    static data members, 50
    static initializers, 51
    static methods, 50
    variable-length argument lists
            (varargs), 48
ObjectInputStream class, 125
ObjectOutputStream class, 125
objects, 41–48
    accessing data members and
            methods in, 43
    cloning, 38
    constructors, 45
    creating, 42
    defined, 41
    serializing and deserializing
            (see serialization)
    this keyword, 47
OOP (see object-oriented pro-
        gramming)
operators, 12
    for binary promotion rules, 25

Oracle
    command-line tools, 102
    JDK (Java Development Kit),
            100
org.ietf.jgss, 95
org.omg.CORBA, 94
org.omg.CORBA_2_3, 94
org.w3c.dom, 97
org.xml.sax, 97
out stream, 120
OutOfMemoryError, 69, 117
output (see input and output)
output streams, 120
overloading methods, 43
@Override annotation, 53
overriding methods, 44

P

package-private modifier, 79, 100
packages
    Java program packager, 106
    names, 5
    representation in UML, 179
parallel compacting garbage col-
        lector, 112
parallel garbage collector, 112
parameter names, 4
Path interface, 129
PathMatcher interface, 131
positive infinity, 22
primitive types, 19
    automatic conversion between
            wrapper classes and, 26
    comparison to reference types,
            30
    literals for, 20
    numeric promotion of, 24
    passing into methods, 34
    wrapper classes, 26
printable ASCII characters, 8
printf( ) method, 48
printStackTrace( ) method, 76
PrintWriter class, 122, 124

priorities (thread), 135
PriorityQueue class, 144, 146
private modifier, 79, 80
programs
    Java program packager, 106
    Java program structure, 100
protected modifier, 79, 80
public modifier, 79, 80
PushbackInputStream class, 122

Q

Queue interface, 143

R

RandomAccessFile class, 128
raw types, generic methods in, 154
readers, 120
reference types, 29–39
    comparing, 35
        != operator, 35
        == operator, 35
        enumerations, 37
        equals( ) method, 35
        strings, 36
    comparison to primitive types, 30
    conversions, 32
    converting between primitives and, 33
    copying, 38
        cloning objects, 38
        reference to an object, 38
    default values
        arrays, 31
        instance and local variables, 30
    memory allocation and garbage collection, 39
    passing into methods, 33
    wrapper classes for primitive types, 26
        autoboxing and unboxing, 26

Remote Method Invocation (RMI) libraries, 93
REPLACE_EXISTING, 131
Retention meta-annotation, 54
return statement, 61
RMI (Remote Method Invocation) libraries, 93
RUNNABLE (thread state), 134
Runnable interface, 133
    implementing, 134
Runtime.getRuntime( ).gc( ) method, 118
RuntimeException class, 66, 75

S

ScheduledThreadPoolExecutor class, 138
ScriptEngine interface, 157
ScriptEngineManager class, 157
Scripting API (see Java Scripting API)
scripting languages, 157
    JSR-223 compatible, 171
    setup, 160
scripts
    accessing and controlling Java resources from, 159
    embedding into Java, 157
security libraries, 94
seeking in files, 128
separators, 12
sequence diagrams (UML), 183
    activation bar, 184
    asynchronous message, 184
    found message, 183
    lifeline, 184
    message to self (self-call), 184
    participant, 183
    synchronous message, 183
serial garbage collector, 112
Serializable interface, 125
serialization, 125

Set interface, 143
    methods, 144
shallow cloning, 39
single line comments, 9
single value annotations, 54
Socket class, 123
socket reading and writing (see input and output)
source files, 100
SQLException, 68
StackOverflowError, 69
statements, 55–63
    assert, 62
    blocks, 56
    conditional, 56–58
        if else if statement, 57
        if else statement, 57
        if statement, 56
        switch statement, 58
    empty, 56
    exception handling, 63
    expression, 55
    iteration, 58–60
        do while loop, 60
        enhanced for loop, 59
        for loop, 59
        while loop, 59
    synchronized, 62, 82
    transfer of control, 60
        break statement, 60
        continue statement, 61
        return statement, 61
static constants, 51
static data members, 50
static initializers, 51
static keyword, 50
static methods, 50
    calibrate( ), with synchronized lock, 137
static modifier, 79, 81
static variable names, 4
strictfp modifier, 79, 81
string literals, 15

strings, comparing, 36
subclasses, 46
Substitution Principle, 151
super keyword, 46
super wildcard, 152
superclasses, 41, 46
@SuppressWarnings annotation, 53
Swing API
    user interface libraries, 91
switch statement, 58
synchronization, 136
synchronized keyword, 62, 136
synchronized modifier, 79, 82
synchronized statement, 62
synchronizers, 140
System.err, 120
System.gc( ) method, 118
System.in, 119
System.out, 120

T

temporary variable names, 4
TERMINATED (thread state), 134
test tools, third-party, 165
text editors, 100
third-party tools, 165–173
    development, CM, and test tools, 165
    scripting languages, 171
    web application platforms, 170
this keyword, 47
    object instance with synchronized lock, 137
Thread class, 133
    commonly used methods, 135
    extending, 133
    static methods for threads, 136
thread-safe equivalents of collection classes, 139
Thread.state enumeration, 134
ThreadPoolExecutor class, 138

threads, 133–141
  common methods used for, 135
  creating, 133
  priorities, 135
throw keyword, 63, 70
Throwable class, 65
time efficiencies, Bit O notation, 147
TIMED_WAITING (thread state), 134
TimeUnit enumeration, 140
toString( ) method, information about exceptions, 76
transfer of control statements, 60
  break, 60
  continue, 61
  return, 61
transient modifier, 79, 82, 125
TreeMap class, 144, 146
TreeSet class, 144, 146
try keyword, 70
try-catch statement, 71
try-catch-finally statement, 73
try-finally statement, 72
try-with-resources statement, 73
try/catch/finally keywords, 63, 70
type parameter within angular brackets (generics), 149
type parameters, bounds, and wildcards, 152

U

UI (user interface) libraries
  AWT (Abstract Window Toolkit) API, 90
  miscellaneous, 90
  Swing API, 91
UML (Unified Modeling Language) basics, 175–184
  class diagrams, 175–177
  class relationships, 181
  connectors, 179
  graphical icon representation, 178
    classes, abstract classes, and interfaces, 178
    notes, 179
    packages, 179
  multiplicity indicators, 180
  object diagrams, 177
  role names, 180
  sequence diagrams, 183
unary numeric promotion (primitive types), 24
unboxing, 28
unchecked exceptions, 66
  common, 68
uncompressing GZIP files, 126
Unicode, 7
  currency symbols, 17
unzipping files, 126
utility libraries, 86

V

variable-length argument lists (varargs), 48–49
Vector class, 144
VirtualMachineError, 69
volatile modifier, 79, 82

W

WAITING (thread state), 134
WatchService interface, 131
web application platforms, 170
while loop, 59
widening conversions, 32
wildcards, applied to type parameters, 152
  best usage of extends and super wildcards, 152
wrapper classes for primitive types, 26
  automatic conversion between primitive types and, 26
writers, 120

X

XML libraries, 95
–XX options for JVM, no guarantee of stability, 114

Z

ZIP files, 126
ZipInputStream class, 126
ZipOutputStream class, 126

The information you need, when and where you need it.

With Safari Books Online, you can:

Access the contents of thousands of technology and business books

- Quickly search over 7000 books and certification guides
- Download whole books or chapters in PDF format, at no extra cost, to print or read on the go
- Copy and paste code
- Save up to 35% on O'Reilly print books
- **New!** Access mobile-friendly books directly from cell phones and mobile devices

Stay up-to-date on emerging topics before the books are published

- Get on-demand access to evolving manuscripts.
- Interact directly with authors of upcoming books

Explore thousands of hours of video on technology and design topics

- Learn from expert video tutorials
- Watch and replay recorded conference sessions

O'REILLY®

Get even more for your money.

Join the O'Reilly Community, and register the O'Reilly books you own. It's free, and you'll get:

- $4.99 ebook upgrade offer
- 40% upgrade offer on O'Reilly print books
- Membership discounts on books and events
- Free lifetime updates to ebooks and videos
- Multiple ebook formats, DRM FREE
- Participation in the O'Reilly community
- Newsletters
- Account management
- 100% Satisfaction Guarantee

To order books online:
oreilly.com/store

For questions about products or an order:
orders@oreilly.com

To sign up to get topic-specific email announcements and/or news about upcoming books, conferences, special offers, and new technologies:
elists@oreilly.com

For technical questions about book content:
booktech@oreilly.com

To submit new book proposals to our editors:
proposals@oreilly.com

O'Reilly books are available in multiple DRM-free ebook formats. For more information:
oreilly.com/ebooks

O'REILLY

CPSIA information can be obtained at www.ICGtesting.com
Printed in the USA
BVOW11n1435260114

342905BV00005B/10/P